NO PLACE LIKE HOME
IN PLASTIC CANVAS

Transform your house into a "home sweet home" by decorating with personal, handmade pretties packed with homegrown charm. No Place Like Home in Plastic Canvas *is loaded with wall hangings, baskets, coasters, and more for adding coziness to your quarters. Choose a favorite style — Victorian or rustic, floral or fanciful — to highlight different rooms or moods. Or feature special interests, from bird watching and quilting to golfing and fishing, with our eye-catching adornments. You can even accessorize your home away from home with accent pieces for your camper or motor home! Or for a real treasure, stitch up our goldfish bowl, which features a pirate's chest and underwater castle. To pick your favorites, just turn the pages. You'll find many imaginative items that carry your spirits homeward bound!*

LEISURE ARTS, INC.
and
OXMOOR HOUSE, INC.

NO PLACE LIKE HOME
IN PLASTIC CANVAS

EDITORIAL STAFF

Vice President and Editor-in-Chief: Anne Van Wagner Childs
Executive Director: Sandra Graham Case
Editorial Director: Susan Frantz Wiles
Publications Director: Carla Bentley
Creative Art Director: Gloria Bearden
Senior Graphics Art Director: Melinda Stout

PRODUCTION
Special Projects Editor: Donna Brown Hill
Senior Production Assistant: JoAnn Dickson Forrest
Project Assistants: Lylln Craig, Michelle Goodrich, Christine Street, and Janie Wright

EDITORIAL
Managing Editor: Linda L. Trimble
Associate Editor: Janice Teipen Wojcik
Assistant Editors: Terri Leming Davidson and Stacey Robertson Marshall

DESIGN
Design Director: Patricia Wallenfang Sowers
Designers: Sandra Spotts Ritchie and Cherece Athy-Watson

ART
Crafts Art Director: Rhonda Hodge Shelby
Senior Production Artist: Katie Murphy
Production Artists: Keith Melton, Brent Miller, Dana Vaughn, Mary Ellen Wilhelm, and Karen L. Wilson
Photography Stylists: Beth Carter, Pam Choate, Aurora Huston, Laura Reed, and Courtney Jones

PROMOTIONS
Managing Editors: Alan Caudle and Marjorie Ann Lacy
Associate Editors: Debby Carr, Ellen J. Clifton, Steve M. Cooper, Dixie L. Morris, and Beth Stark
Art Director: Linda Lovette Smart
Publishing Systems Administrator: Cindy Lumpkin
Publishing Systems Assistants: Susan Mary Gray and Robert Walker

BUSINESS STAFF

Publisher: Rick Barton
Vice President and General Manager: Thomas L. Carlisle
Vice President, Finance: Tom Siebenmorgen
Vice President, Retail Marketing: Bob Humphrey
Vice President, National Accounts: Pam Stebbins
Retail Marketing Director: Margaret Sweetin
General Merchandise Manager: Cathy Laird

Vice President, Operations: Brian U. Davis
Distribution Director: Rob Thieme
Retail Customer Service Director: Tonie B. Maulding
Retail Customer Service Managers: Carolyn Pruss and Wanda Price
Print Production Manger: Fred F. Pruss

Library of Congress Catalog Number 98-65609
Hardcover ISBN 1-57486-139-5
Softcover ISBN 1-57486-145-X

TABLE OF CONTENTS

Bless Our Home

With colorful blooming window boxes, brightly lit windows, and a beribboned door wreath, our stately Williamsburg dwelling (below) delivers a comfortable, homey feeling. The home is charming either as a bookend or a doorstop. Inspired by vintage needlepoint, our pretty framed piece (opposite) is designed to attract added blessings to your home! Coordinating coasters and candle band complete the lovely floral set.

Instructions on pages 34-37

O Give Me A Home

Home on the range — this legendary locale evokes images of hearty pioneers and rugged frontier living. Bring the robust feeling of this bygone era into your little cabin in the woods with decorations inspired by our forefathers' homespun simplicity. Bear and deer roam freely across our diamond-patterned rug (below), which is stitched on 5 mesh canvas. Our rustic log cabin (opposite), complete with a stone chimney, is quite versatile. Use it as a tissue box cover or as a box to store anything from candy, potpourri, or notepads to our attractive quilt pattern coasters.

Instructions on pages 38-43

A House & A Tree

Our fine feathered friends and their brightly hued dwellings bring the pleasure of bird watching indoors. As refreshing as a springtime breeze, our whimsical birdhouse magnets (below) are highlighted with perky flowers. A grapevine wreath accented with silk blossoms, ivy, and a raffia bow (opposite) is a natural perch for an eye-catching goldfinch, cardinal, and bluebird.

Instructions on pages 44-45

9

It's easy to create a charming window brightener when you start with a store-bought birdhouse, then add our colorful three-dimensional songbird and a floral accent. This stay-at-home goldfinch, whose plumage is offset by black and white markings, promises to perk up any nook or cranny that becomes his home.

Two rose-breasted bluebirds extend a "heart-y" hello to all your guests on our pretty pastel "Welcome" banner (left). This sign signals the arrival of visitors with little liberty bells dangling on grosgrain ribbons. Fill a quiet corner with the sweet scent of potpourri and the striking scarlet of our three-dimensional cardinal (below, left). Accurately detailed, right down to his pointed cap and distinctive black markings, this handsome bird graces a "nest" highlighted with crimson berries and a rosebud. Our decorative mini birdhouse (below, right) gives a touch of the great outdoors to indoor habitats such as your office, kitchen, or den.

Instructions on pages 45-47

Be It Ever So Humble

Our out-of-the ordinary pets add a homey touch to any dwelling! A shiny goldfish (below) swims in an "underwater" paradise complete with castle and treasure chest. Metallic yarn and sparkling acrylic "jewels" give the designs a shimmering effect. Our self-assured calico kitty (opposite) keeps track of your keys — even if everything else is in a jumble! Drapery hooks serve as key holders, and stitching with two strands of yarn gives Tabby his textured look.

Instructions on pages 48-50

13

Home Is Where
The Heart Can Bloom

Bring old-fashioned charm into your household with our collection of "heart-y" blooms. Accented with silk flowers, our wall pocket (below) is cleverly fashioned from two plastic canvas pieces — one heart-shaped and the other square. As pretty as a picture in a storybook, our Victorian cottage tissue box cover (opposite) sports charming details such as silk flowers in window boxes, a heart-embellished picket fence, and "smoke" rising from the chimney.

Instructions on pages 51-54

15

Surround yourself with sweet sentiments by decorating with heart-shaped blossoms. Display a favorite photo in our hearts and flowers frame (below) to show your affection for a loved one. To create the matching doily, stitch four heart-shaped plastic canvas pieces together. Carry this delicate pattern throughout the house with a flowerpot cover (opposite), a welcoming door hanger, and potpourri-filled sachet cubes.

Instructions on pages 55-57

Home Is Where The Heart Can Rest

Lend a cozy feel to your favorite corner with the ageless appeal of the quilter's art. Our doll-sized bed (below) with its classic coverlet *is more than just a pretty accent piece! Lift the blanket to discover a dust ruffle-edged box storing "quilts" that double as coasters. Three patchwork designs are stitched twice to make the six coasters. Nine popular patterns are displayed on our sampler* (opposite), *which is worked in soothing shades of blue.*

Instructions on pages 58-61

19

What a crafty idea! Our quilt-patterned jewelry box (right) opens to reveal a foldout holder for earrings, pins, and other accessories. A handy carrier for fragrant potpourri, bath salts, washcloths, or soaps, our bath basket (below) is decorated with appealing patchwork patterns. The set also features a basket that's perfect for daily necessities (opposite, clockwise from lower left), a tissue box cover stitched on almond canvas, and a mug with a quilt-block insert.

Instructions on pages 58-60 and 62-63

God Bless Our Country Home

Sweetened with berries and flowers, our charming bee skep (below) adds a pleasant touch to your country home. Both practical and pleasing, the whimsical farm scene (opposite) features a happy-go-lucky farmer and a barnyard full of endearing animals. The photo inset reveals ingenious spots that cleverly conceal desktop items. You'll find tissues in the hayloft, a ruler in the silo, a notepad in the barn door, stationery in the toolshed, and a pencil in the milk can!

Instructions on pages 64-71

23

Spread homespun goodness throughout your kitchen with colorful "down home" accents like our miniature barn (right) *and cheery farm-fresh magnets* (below). *For awesome gifts and table brighteners, combine yummy creations from your kitchen with charming jar lids* (opposite, top) *that show off a curly tailed pig, a heartwarming sentiment for the cook, and bees buzzing atop a honeycomb. The "Fresh Eggs" sign* (opposite, bottom) *has an interesting shadow-box effect created by sandwiching fabric-covered cardboard between plastic canvas pieces.*

Instructions on pages 65-66 and 72-73

25

Home Away from Home

Hit the high road in style with our recreational vehicle tissue box cover (below)! Perfect for your home away from home, this detailed design has the tissue opening tucked in back (shown on page 28). Enjoy the allure of fishing — even when the fish refuse to bite — by hanging up our trout trio (opposite). A terrific catch at any time, the string of fish is a crafty reminder of productive days at the lake or stream.

Instructions on pages 74-77

Add personality to your travel home with pretty, practical pieces that reflect your lifestyle. Coasters shaped like recreational vehicles (below) are housed in a stand-up holder featuring a mountain scene. The coordinating tissue box cover is equipped with a ladder and wheels made from plastic canvas circles. Display your love for the links with pencil toppers that look like miniature golf club covers. A cute golf bag keeps the pencils within easy reach. Get organized with magnets modeled after popular camper styles (opposite)— complete with black button "wheels." The set even has a sign declaring your fluency in camping lingo!

Instructions on pages 74-79

Happiness Is Homegrown

Flavorful farm-fresh produce, the bounty of summer, inspired our true-to-life veggie magnets (below). These will make crafty, homegrown additions to your country kitchen. Arranged in neat little rows, sun-ripened vegetables are a charming touch on our roadside stand tissue box cover (right). Just above the lettuce and tomatoes is a clever opening that keeps tissues close at hand.

Instructions on pages 80-83

31

East-West, Home Is Best

Infuse your home with the spirit of the Southwest and its spectacular sunsets by decorating with our engaging accents. Highlighted with cacti and Native American pottery, this adobe village (below and inset) *is an eye-catching conversation piece. The unique frame* (opposite), *which brings an intriguing touch to table, shelf, or mantel, achieves its textured effect with yarn-covered cording. Coordinating coasters have a variegated look created by stitching two or three tones of pastel yarn on precut plastic canvas shapes.*

Instructions on pages 84-90

Bless Our Home

TOWNHOUSE DOORSTOP/BOOKEND

(Shown on page 4)

Size: 4³/₄"w x 10³/₄"h x 3"d

Supplies: Worsted weight yarn, two 10¹/₂" x 13¹/₂" sheets of clear 7 mesh plastic canvas, #16 tapestry needle, 3¹/₂"w x 7¹/₂"h x 2¹/₈"d brick, plastic wrap, assorted miniature silk flowers and greenery, 12" length of purple ribbon, and craft glue

Stitches Used: Backstitch, French Knot, Gobelin Stitch, Overcast Stitch, Scotch Stitch, and Tent Stitch

Instructions: Follow charts to cut and stitch pieces. Cut a 27 x 52 thread piece of plastic canvas for Box Front. Cut a 27 x 17 thread piece of plastic canvas for Bottom. Front and Bottom are not stitched.

With wrong sides facing inward, join long edges of Back to Sides using dk rose yarn. Join Front to Sides. Join Top to Front, Back, and Sides.

Wrap brick with plastic wrap and insert brick into Doorstop/Bookend. Join Bottom to Front, Back, and Sides.

Glue flowers and Window Boxes to Townhouse. Wrap ribbon around Wreath; trim and glue ends to Wreath. Glue flowers to Wreath. Glue Wreath to door. Glue Townhouse to Box Front.

Design by Michele Wilcox.

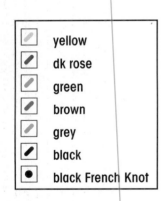

◪	yellow
◪	dk rose
◪	green
◪	brown
◪	grey
◪	black
⊙	black French Knot

Townhouse

(31 x 71 threads)

Wreath

(8 x 8 threads)

Window Box

(11 x 5 threads)

(stitch 5)

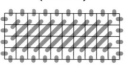

Box Top

(27 x 17 threads)

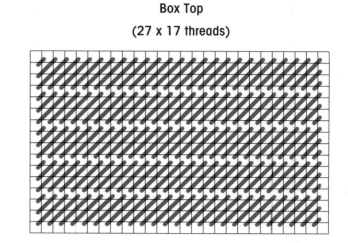

Box Side

(17 x 52 threads) (stitch 2)

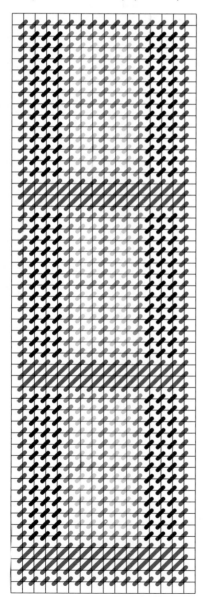

Box Back

(27 x 52 threads)

ROSE COASTER

(Shown on page 5)

Size: 4¹/₂"w x 4¹/₂"h

Supplies for One Coaster: Worsted weight yarn, 10¹/₂" x 13¹/₂" sheet of clear 7 mesh plastic canvas, #16 tapestry needle, cork or felt (optional), and craft glue (optional)

Stitches Used: Overcast Stitch and Tent Stitch

Instructions: Follow chart to cut and stitch design. Complete background with black Tent Stitches as shown on chart. Using black yarn, cover unworked edges of Coaster.

If desired, cut a piece of cork or felt slightly smaller than Coaster. Glue cork or felt to back of Coaster.

VIOLET CANDLE BAND

(Shown on page 5)

Size: 3¹/₄" dia.

(Fits a 2³/₄" dia. pillar candle.)

Supplies: Worsted weight yarn, one 10¹/₂" x 13¹/₂" sheet of clear 7 mesh plastic canvas, and #16 tapestry needle

Stitches Used: Overcast Stitch and Tent Stitch

Instructions: Follow chart to cut and stitch design. Complete background with black Tent Stitches as shown on chart. Using black yarn, join short edges of stitched piece together to form a cylinder. Cover unworked edges of Candle Band.

"BLESS OUR HOME" FRAMED PIECE

(Shown on page 5)

Size: 15"w x 12¹/₄"h

Supplies: Worsted weight yarn, one 13¹/₂" x 22" sheet of clear 7 mesh plastic canvas, and #16 tapestry needle

Stitches Used: Overcast Stitch and Tent Stitch

Instructions: Follow chart to cut and stitch design. Complete background with black Tent Stitches as shown on chart. "Bless Our Home" is custom framed.

Designs by Kathleen Hurley.

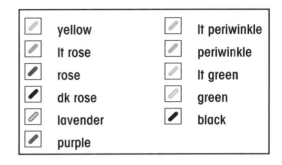

✎	yellow	✎	lt periwinkle
✎	lt rose	✎	periwinkle
✎	rose	✎	lt green
✎	dk rose	✎	green
✎	lavender	✎	black
✎	purple		

Coaster

(30 x 30 threads)

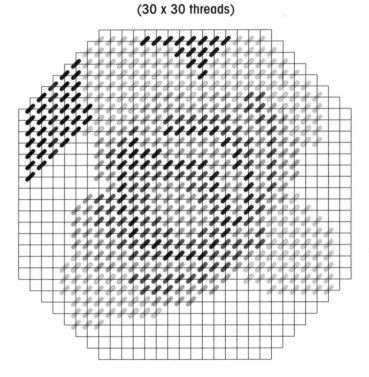

Candle Band (66 x 17 threads)

36

"Bless Our Home" (82 x 101 threads)

O Give Me A Home

LOG CABIN BOX
(Shown on page 7)

Size: 6"w x 9"h x 7"d
(Fits a 4¼"w x 5¼"h x 4¼"d boutique tissue box.)

Supplies: Worsted weight yarn, four 10½" x 13½" sheets of clear 7 mesh stiff plastic canvas, #16 tapestry needle, and craft glue

Stitches Used: Gobelin Stitch, Overcast Stitch, Padded Satin Stitch, and Tent Stitch

Instructions: Follow charts to cut and stitch pieces.

Using various colors of yarn, join Chimney Front to Chimney Side #1 between ★'s. Join Chimney Front to Chimney Side #2 between ▲'s. Join Chimney Back to Chimney Side #1 between ✖'s. Join Chimney Back to Chimney Side #2 between ■'s. Center and glue Chimney Back to one cabin Side piece.

Using rust yarn, join one long edge of Front to one Side piece. Repeat to join Front to remaining Side piece. Join Back to Sides.

For tissue box cover, cover unworked edges with rust yarn. For storage box, cut a 33 x 33 thread piece of plastic canvas for Bottom. Bottom is not stitched. Join Bottom to Front, Back, and Sides.

Using dk brown yarn, join unworked edges of Roof pieces together. Glue one Roof piece to Log Cabin. (Remaining Roof piece lifts for tissue removal or for storage.)

Design by Trish Suder.

PADDED SATIN STITCH
This stitch is worked in two steps. First, work horizontal stitches as shown in **Fig. 1**. Then work vertical stitches over the horizontal stitches **(Fig. 2)**.

Fig. 1

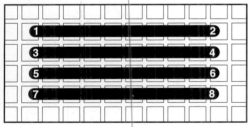

Fig. 2

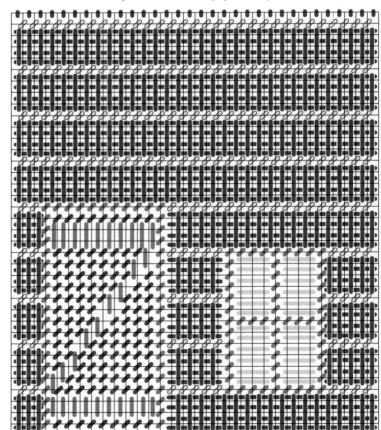

Diagram

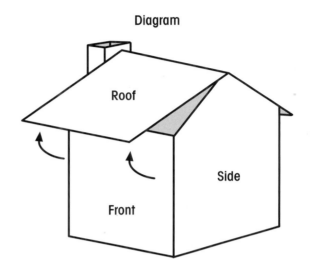

Front/Back

(33 x 38 threads) (stitch 2)

38

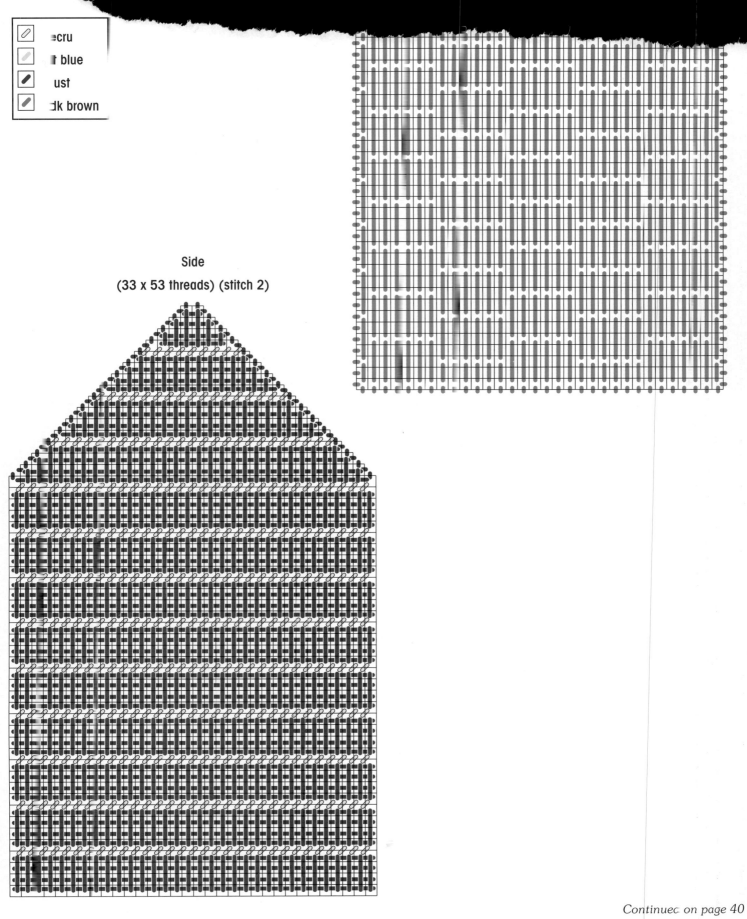

	ecru
	lt blue
	rust
	dk brown

Side
(33 x 53 threads) (stitch 2)

Continued on page 40

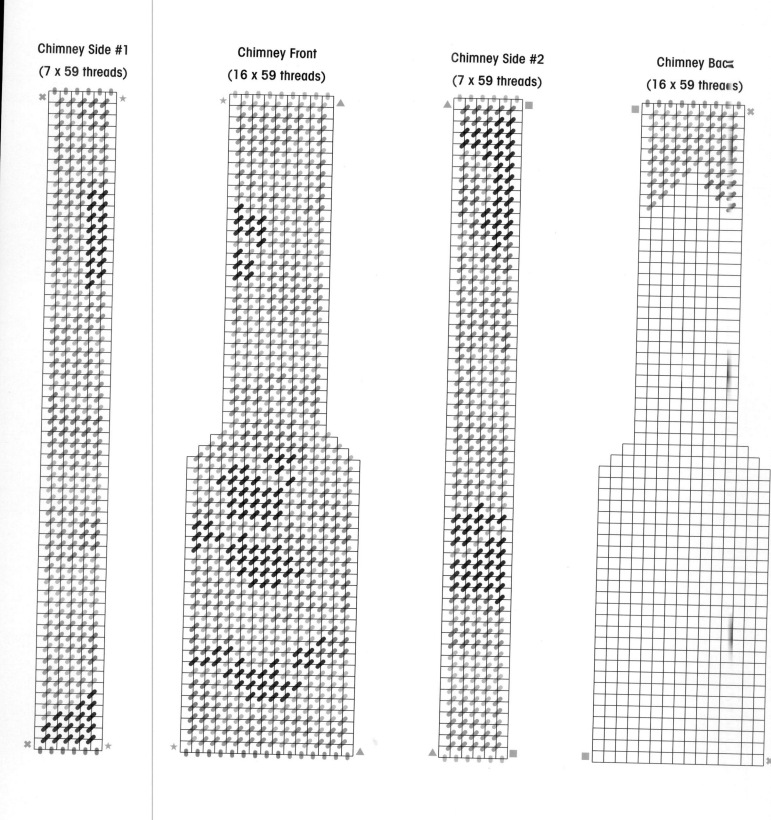

tan   lt grey

Chimney Side #1
(7 x 59 threads)

Chimney Front
(16 x 59 threads)

Chimney Side #2
(7 x 59 threads)

Chimney Back
(16 x 59 threads)

RUSTIC COASTER

(Shown on page 7)

Size: 4¼"w x 4¼"h

Supplies for One Coaster: Worsted weight yarn, 10½" x 13½" sheet of clear 7 mesh plastic canvas, #16 tapestry needle, cork or felt (optional), and craft glue (optional)

Stitches Used: Gobelin Stitch, Overcast Stitch, Scotch Stitch, and Tent Stitch

Instructions: Follow chart to cut and stitch Coaster. If desired, cut a piece of cork or felt slightly smaller than Coaster. Glue cork or felt to back of Coaster.

RUSTIC RUG

(Shown on page 6)

Size: 31"w x 17"h

Supplies: Worsted weight yarn, two 13½" x 22" sheets of clear 5 mesh plastic canvas, #16 tapestry needle, nonskid rug backing (optional), and Scotchgard™ brand fabric protector (optional)

Stitches Used: Fringe Stitch, Overcast Stitch, and Tent Stitch

Instructions: Unless otherwise indicated in color key, use two strands of yarn to work stitches. Follow charts to cut and stitch pieces, leaving stitches in shaded area unworked. Complete background with ecru Tent Stitches as indicated on chart. Trim Fringe to 2½" long.

Matching ★'s, place Right Side on top of Left Side and work stitches in shaded area through both thicknesses of plastic canvas to join pieces together. Complete background in shaded area with ecru Tent Stitches. Using rust yarn, cover unworked edges of Rug.

If desired, follow manufacturer's instructions to apply fabric protector and nonskid rug backing to Rug.

Rug design by Polly Carbonari.

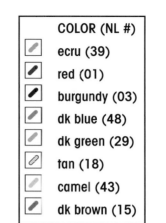

COLOR (NL #)	
	ecru (39)
	red (01)
	burgundy (03)
	dk blue (48)
	dk green (29)
	tan (18)
	camel (43)
	dk brown (15)

Coaster

(28 x 28 threads)

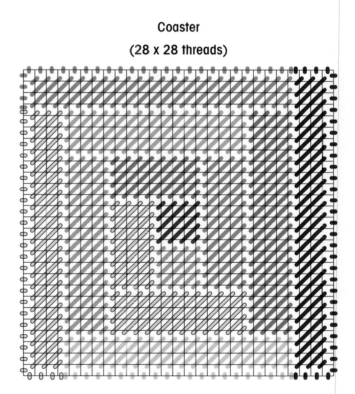

Continued on page 42

COLOR (NL #)	COLOR (NL #)	COLOR (NL #)
ecru (39)	dk blue (48)	dk green (29)
red (01)	green (28)	rust (10)

Left Side (67 x 85 threads)

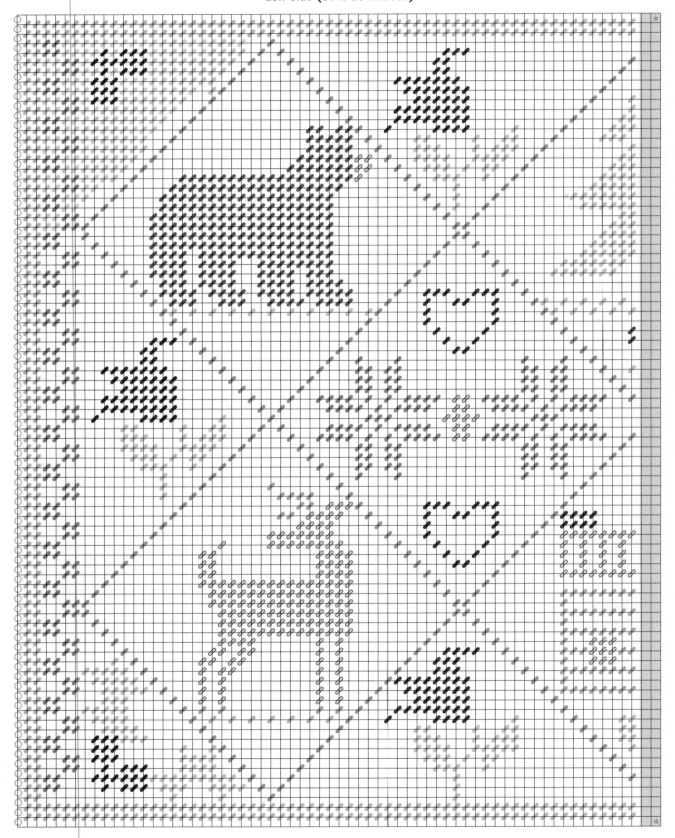

	COLOR (NL #)		COLOR (NL #)		COLOR (NL #)
✎	tan (18)	✎	brown (14)	○	rust Fringe (10) - 1 strand
✎	lt brown (13)	✎	dk brown (15)		

Right Side (67 x 85 threads)

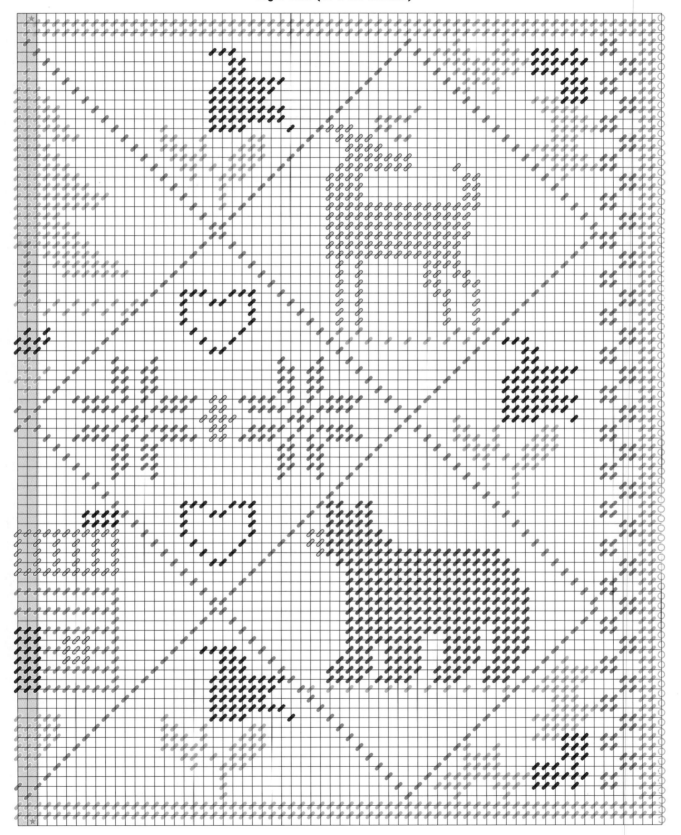

A House & A Tree

BIRDHOUSE MAGNETS

(Shown on page 8)

Approx. Size:
2¹⁄₂"w x 4³⁄₄"h each

Supplies: Worsted weight yarn, embroidery floss, one 10¹⁄₂" x 13¹⁄₂" sheet of clear 7 mesh plastic canvas, #16 tapestry needle, magnetic strip, and craft glue

Stitches Used: Backstitch, Cross Stitch, French Knot, Gobelin Stitch, Mosaic Stitch, Overcast Stitch, and Tent Stitch

Instructions: Follow charts to cut and stitch pieces. Use six strands of embroidery floss for Backstitch. Using matching color yarn, join Birdhouse Fronts to Birdhouse Backs. Cover unworked edges of pieces. Glue pieces to Birdhouses. Glue magnetic strip to back of Birdhouses.

Designs by Becky Dill.

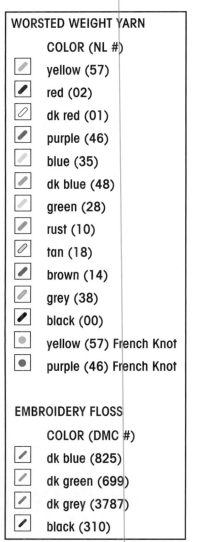

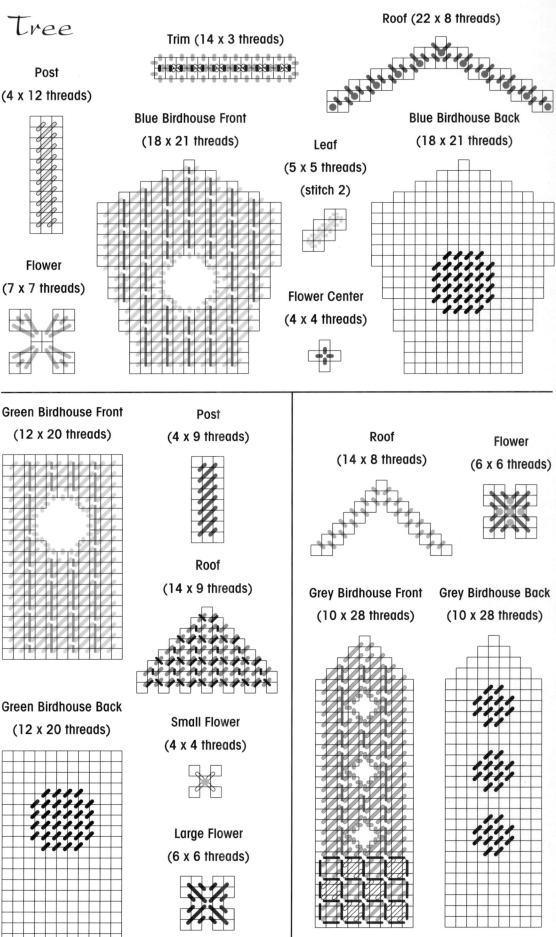

Trim (14 x 3 threads)

Roof (22 x 8 threads)

Post
(4 x 12 threads)

Blue Birdhouse Front
(18 x 21 threads)

Blue Birdhouse Back
(18 x 21 threads)

Leaf
(5 x 5 threads)
(stitch 2)

Flower
(7 x 7 threads)

Flower Center
(4 x 4 threads)

Green Birdhouse Front
(12 x 20 threads)

Post
(4 x 9 threads)

Roof
(14 x 8 threads)

Flower
(6 x 6 threads)

Roof
(14 x 9 threads)

Grey Birdhouse Front
(10 x 28 threads)

Grey Birdhouse Back
(10 x 28 threads)

Small Flower
(4 x 4 threads)

Green Birdhouse Back
(12 x 20 threads)

Large Flower
(6 x 6 threads)

44

BIRD WATCHER'S WREATH

(Shown on page 9)

Size: 16" dia.

Supplies: Worsted weight yarn, one 10½" x 13½" sheet of clear 7 mesh plastic canvas, #16 tapestry needle, 16" dia. grapevine wreath, raffia, silk flowers, artificial ivy, and craft glue

Stitches Used: Backstitch, French Knot, Gobelin Stitch, Overcast Stitch, and Tent Stitch

Instructions: Follow charts to cut and stitch Flat Goldfinch, Flat Cardinal, and Flat Bluebird. Tie raffia into a bow and trim ends. Glue ivy, flowers, birds, and bow to Wreath.

Designs by Dick Martin.

	COLOR (NL #)
	white (41)
	lt yellow (20)
	yellow (57)
	gold (11)
	dk orange (52)
	pink (07)
	dk pink (05)
	red (02)
	dk red (01)
	blue (35)
	tan (18)
	grey (38)
	black (00)
	tan (18) French Knot
	black (00) French Knot

MINIATURE BIRDHOUSE

(Shown on page 11)

Size: 3½"w x 2½"h x 2¾"d

Supplies: Worsted weight yarn, one 10½" x 13½" sheet of clear 7 mesh plastic canvas, #16 tapestry needle, 10" wooden skewer, dk red paint (optional), and craft glue

Stitches Used: Gobelin Stitch, Overcast Stitch, and Tent Stitch

Instructions: Follow charts to cut and stitch pieces. For Back, cut and stitch a Front piece, omitting opening. For Sides, cut two pieces of plastic canvas 12 x 9 threads each. For Bottom, cut a piece of plastic canvas 12 x 8 threads. Cover Back, Side, and Bottom pieces with blue Tent Stitches.

Using dk red yarn, join Roof pieces together along unworked edges. Join Trim pieces together.

Using blue yarn, join Front to Bottom. Join Back to Bottom. Join Sides to Bottom. Join Sides to Front and Back.

Glue Roof and Trim to Birdhouse. Cut a 2" length of skewer. If desired, paint skewer. Insert skewer into Birdhouse Front.

Design by Terry A. Ricioli.

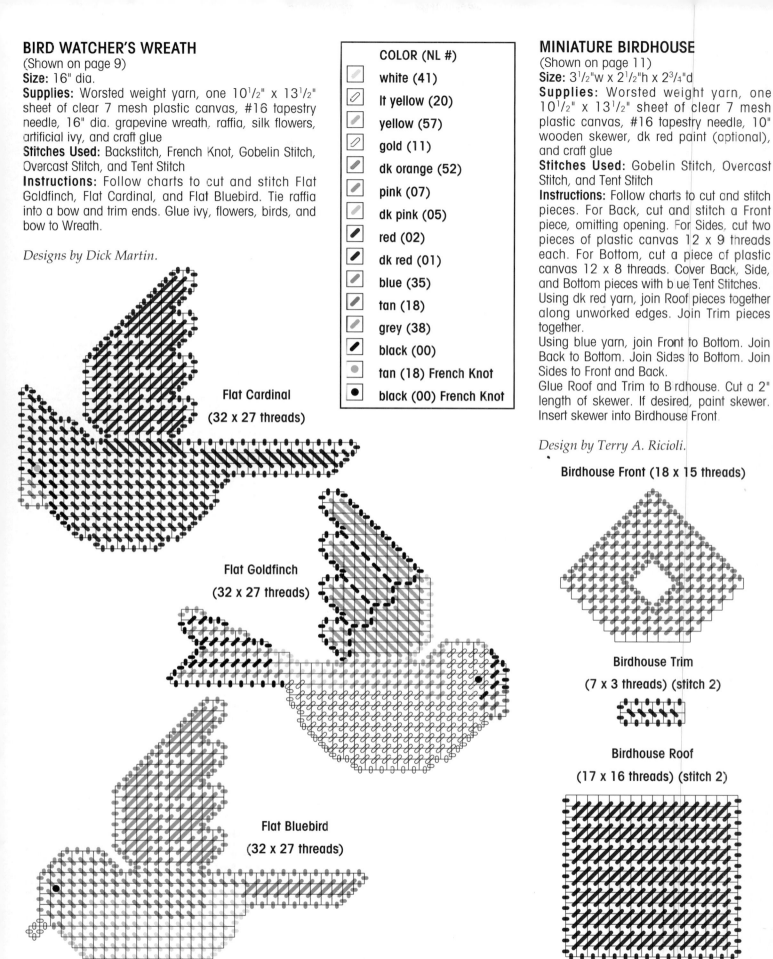

Flat Cardinal
(32 x 27 threads)

Flat Goldfinch
(32 x 27 threads)

Flat Bluebird
(32 x 27 threads)

Birdhouse Front (18 x 15 threads)

Birdhouse Trim
(7 x 3 threads) (stitch 2)

Birdhouse Roof
(17 x 16 threads) (stitch 2)

45

GOLDFINCH AND CARDINAL

(Shown on pages 10 and 11)

Size: 5¼"w x 2¾"h x 5½"d each

Supplies for One Bird: Worsted weight yarn, one 10½" x 13½" sheet of clear 7 mesh plastic canvas, and #16 tapestry needle

Stitches Used: Backstitch, French Knot, Gobelin Stitch, Overcast Stitch, and Tent Stitch

Instructions: Follow charts to cut and stitch Side, Back, and Bottom pieces. Refer to photo for yarn colors used and match symbols to join pieces together. Join Side #1 to Side #2 between ▲'s. Join Sides to Bottom between ◆'s and ■'s. Join Back to unworked edges of Sides and Bottom between ♥'s and ★'s.

Designs by Dick Martin.

COLOR (NL #)	COLOR (NL #)
white (41)	grey (38)
lt yellow (20)	black (00)
yellow (57)	black (00) French Knot
tan (18)	

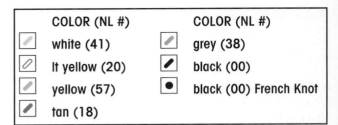

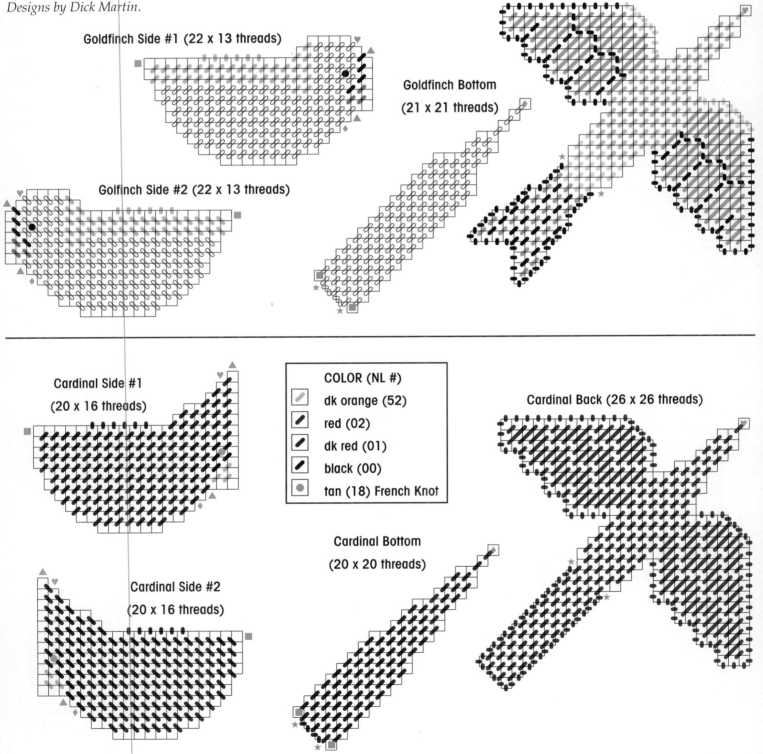

Goldfinch Side #1 (22 x 13 threads)

Golfinch Side #2 (22 x 13 threads)

Goldfinch Bottom (21 x 21 threads)

Goldfinch Back (27 x 27 threads)

Cardinal Side #1 (20 x 16 threads)

Cardinal Side #2 (20 x 16 threads)

Cardinal Bottom (20 x 20 threads)

Cardinal Back (26 x 26 threads)

COLOR (NL #)	
dk orange (52)	
red (02)	
dk red (01)	
black (00)	
tan (18) French Knot	

46

"WELCOME" BANNER

(Shown on page 11)

Size: 11"w x 17¹⁄₂"h

Supplies: Worsted weight yarn, embroidery floss, one 10¹⁄₂" x 13¹⁄₂" sheet of clear 7 mesh plastic canvas, #16 tapestry needle, three 1¹⁄₂" gold liberty bells, one yd of ⁷⁄₈"w grosgrain ribbon, sawtooth hanger, and craft glue

Stitches Used: Backstitch, French Knot, Gobelin Stitch, Modified Eyelet Stitch, Mosaic Stitch, Overcast Stitch, Scotch Stitch, and Tent Stitch

Instructions: Follow chart to cut and stitch Banner. Cut one 10" and two 8" lengths of ribbon. Fold each ribbon end to form a point; glue in place. Glue one bell to back of each ribbon. Glue remaining ribbon ends to back of Banner. Glue sawtooth hanger to back of Banner.

Design by Dick Martin.

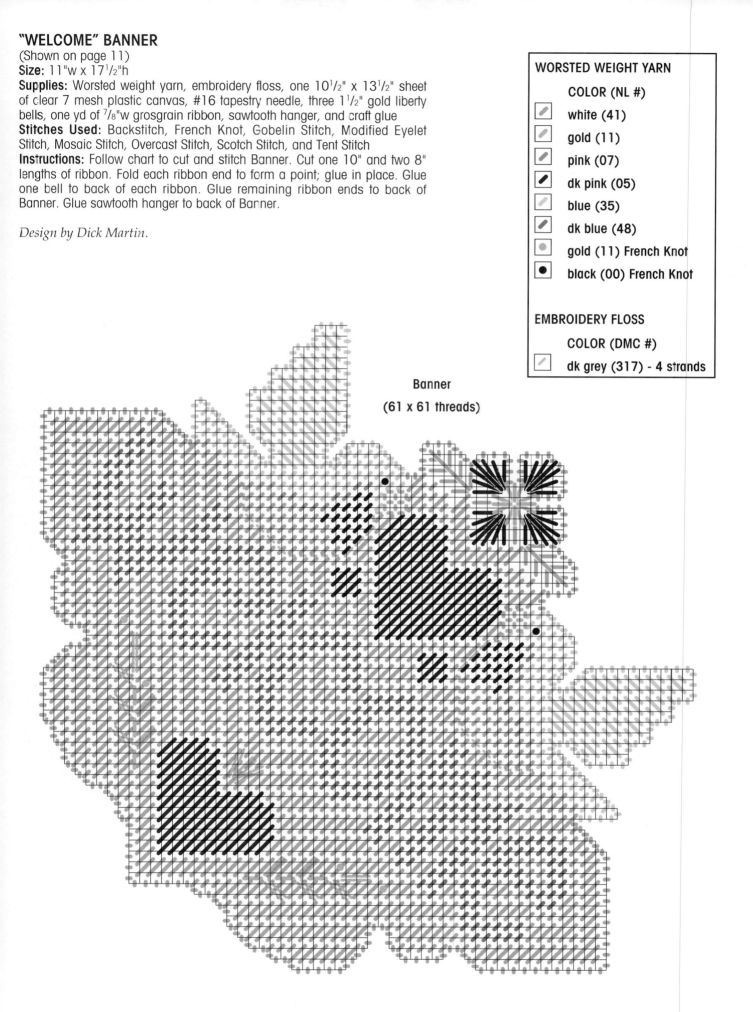

WORSTED WEIGHT YARN	
COLOR (NL #)	
⟋	white (41)
⟋	gold (11)
⟋	pink (07)
⟋	dk pink (05)
⟋	blue (35)
⟋	dk blue (48)
●	gold (11) French Knot
●	black (00) French Knot

EMBROIDERY FLOSS	
COLOR (DMC #)	
⟋	dk grey (317) - 4 strands

Banner

(61 x 61 threads)

Be It Ever So Humble

FISHBOWL

(Shown on page 12)

Size: 5¼"w x 5½"h x 3½"d

Supplies: Kreinik™ Medium (#16) Braid; one 8" x 11" sheet of clear 14 mesh plastic canvas; one 8" x 11" sheet of brown 14 mesh plastic canvas; #24 tapestry needle; 5¼"w x 5½"h x 3½"d fishbowl; 1¼"w x 5"h piece of tan felt; 2-3" lengths of gold metallic cord, silver metallic cord, and string of pearl beads; assorted jewelry findings (glass beads or rhinestones and jump rings); five pound bag of desired color aquarium gravel; disposable plastic container and spoon; window cleaner and paper towel; straight pins; and jewel glue

Stitches Used: Braided Cross Stitch, Gobelin Stitch, Overcast Stitch, Smyrna Cross Stitch, and Tent Stitch

Instructions: Follow charts to cut Castle and Chest pieces from brown plastic canvas. Cut a 21 x 10 thread piece of brown plastic canvas for Chest Bottom. Chest Bottom is not stitched. Cut Seaweed and Goldfish pieces from clear plastic canvas. Stitch Castle Back through both thicknesses of plastic canvas. Stitch remaining Fishbowl pieces.

With wrong sides facing inward, join long edges of one Tower Front piece to two Tower Side pieces using golden sand braid. Repeat with remaining Tower Front and Tower Side pieces. Join one Tower Side piece to Castle Back along green shaded thread through three thicknesses of plastic canvas. Join opposite Tower Side to Castle Back along purple shaded area. Join remaining unworked edges of Castle Back to Tower Sides.

For Chest handles, thread a 3" length of black braid through one Chest Side at ✳'s. Tie knots on back of Side and trim ends. Repeat for remaining Side. Using black braid, join Chest Front to Sides. Join Back to Sides. Join Bottom to Front, Back, and Sides. Join Chest Top to Top Edges between ▲'s. Join remaining unworked edge of Chest Top to Back. Cover remaining unworked edges of Chest. Fold and glue felt inside Chest. Glue cord, pearl beads, and jewelry findings inside chest.

Matching ★'s, tack Fin #1 to Goldfish Front using antique gold braid. Matching ■'s, tack Fin #2 to Goldfish Back. Using matching color yarn, join Goldfish Front to Back.

Hold Seaweed piece under warm running water for one minute to soften. Curl each section out from center around finger to shape. Allow canvas to dry. Cover edges of Seaweed with Braided Cross Stitch. Roll bottom of Seaweed and tack in place using star green braid. Glue Goldfish to Seaweed.

Lightly coat 1½ cups of gravel with glue. Spoon gravel into bowl, pressing down to pack gravel. Add glue to areas where Seaweed, Chest, and Castle will be placed. Pin Seaweed, Chest, and Castle in place as desired and allow glue to dry. Lightly coat ½ cup gravel with glue. Spoon gravel into bowl around pieces and contour as desired. Clean excess glue on glass with window cleaner and paper towel.

Design by Rosemarie Walter.

COLOR (KREINIK #)		COLOR (KREINIK #)	
black (005HL)		yellow orange (127)	
brown (022)		golden sand (212)	
orange (027)		antique gold (221)	
lemon-lime (054F)		curry (2122)	
watermelon (055F)		star green (9194)	

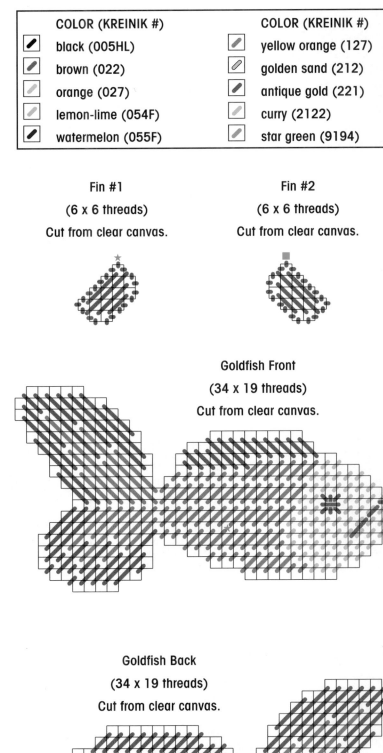

Fin #1
(6 x 6 threads)
Cut from clear canvas.

Fin #2
(6 x 6 threads)
Cut from clear canvas.

Goldfish Front
(34 x 19 threads)
Cut from clear canvas.

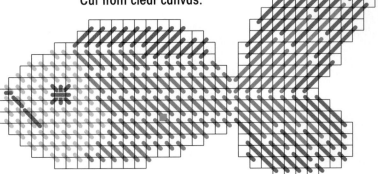

Goldfish Back
(34 x 19 threads)
Cut from clear canvas.

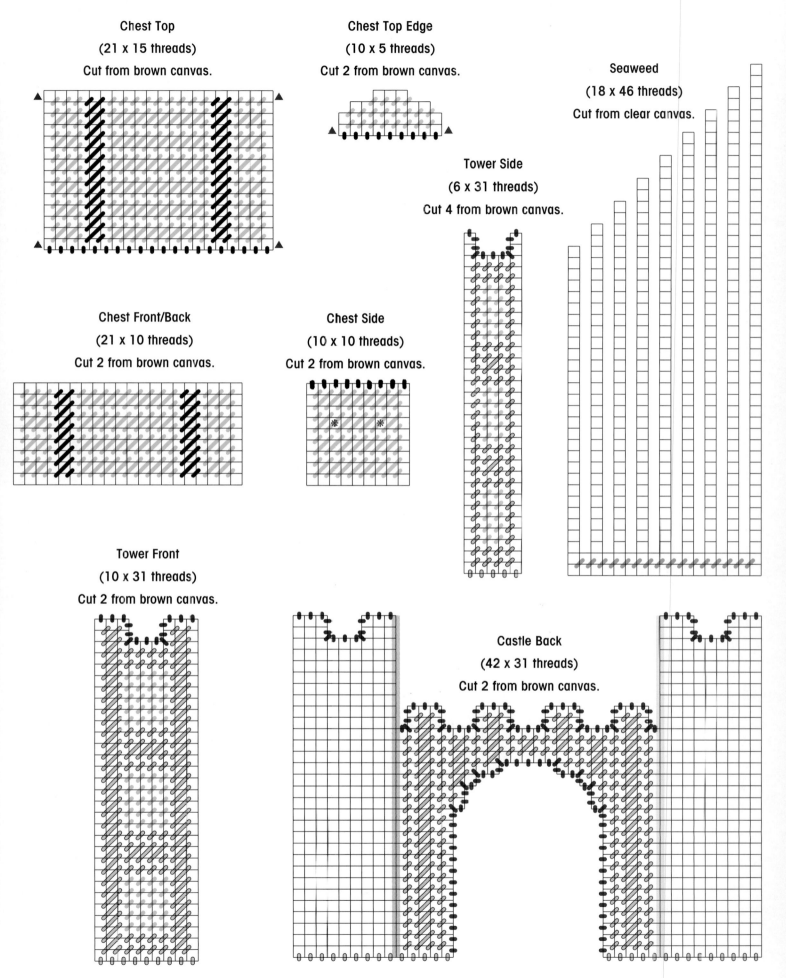

Chest Top

(21 x 15 threads)

Cut from brown canvas.

Chest Top Edge

(10 x 5 threads)

Cut 2 from brown canvas.

Seaweed

(18 x 46 threads)

Cut from clear canvas.

Tower Side

(6 x 31 threads)

Cut 4 from brown canvas.

Chest Front/Back

(21 x 10 threads)

Cut 2 from brown canvas.

Chest Side

(10 x 10 threads)

Cut 2 from brown canvas.

Tower Front

(10 x 31 threads)

Cut 2 from brown canvas.

Castle Back

(42 x 31 threads)

Cut 2 from brown canvas.

KITTEN KEY HOLDER

(Shown on page 13)

Size: 10¼"w x 11¼"h

Supplies: Worsted weight yarn, two 10½" x 13½" sheets of clear 7 mesh plastic canvas, #16 tapestry needle, seven 1½" pin-on drapery hooks, sawtooth hanger, and craft glue

Stitches Used: Backstitch, Cross Stitch, Gobelin Stitch, Overcast Stitch, and Tent Stitch

Instructions: Follow charts to cut and stitch pieces. Matching ■'s, place Rug on top of Kitten and work stitches in green shaded area through both thicknesses of plastic canvas. Cover unworked edges with rust yarn.

Insert one drapery hook at each ▲. Glue Tail to Kitten Key Holder. Glue sawtooth hanger to back of stitched piece.

Design by Dick Martin.

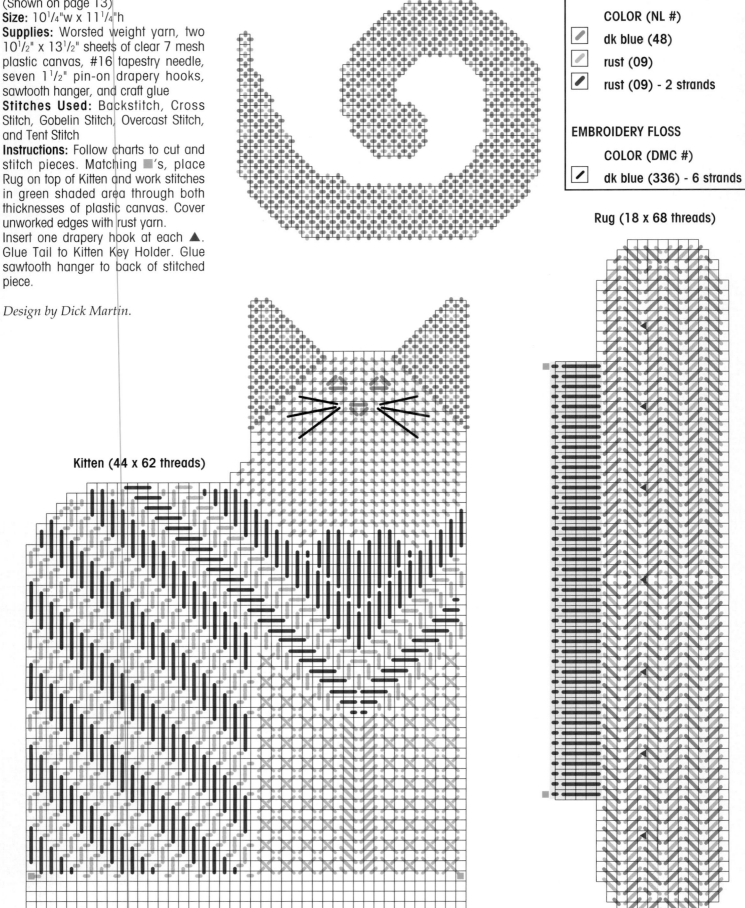

Tail (30 x 24 threads)

Kitten (44 x 62 threads)

Rug (18 x 68 threads)

WORSTED WEIGHT YARN
COLOR (NL #)
dk blue (48)
rust (09)
rust (09) - 2 strands

EMBROIDERY FLOSS
COLOR (DMC #)
dk blue (336) - 6 strands

Home Is Where The Heart Can Bloom

HEART WALL POCKET

(Shown on page 14)

Size: 6¹/₂"w x 6"h

Supplies: Worsted weight yarn, one 10¹/₂" x 13¹/₂" sheet of clear 7 mesh plastic canvas, one Uniek® 6" heart shape, #16 tapestry needle, 10" length of ³/₈"w blue ribbon, and craft glue

Stitches Used: Gobelin Stitch, Mosaic Stitch, Overcast Stitch, and Tent Stitch

Instructions: Follow charts to cut and stitch pieces. Using blue yarn, join Front to Back between ✳'s. Matching ■'s and ▲'s, join Front to Back along unworked edges. Glue ribbon to back of Heart Wall Pocket.

Design by Ann Townsend.

COLOR (NL #)	
	white (41)
	rose (05)
	blue (35)
	green (53)

Heart Pocket Front

(27 x 27 threads)

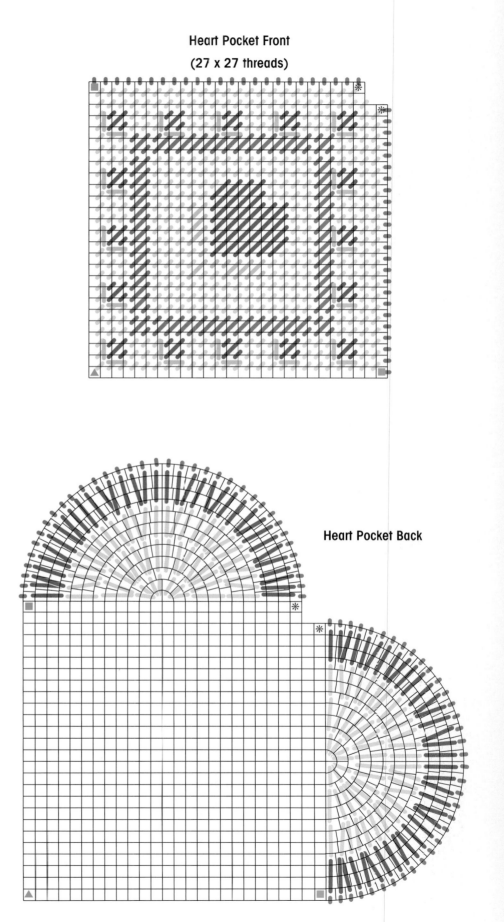

Heart Pocket Back

Home Is Where The Heart Can Bloom

VICTORIAN HOUSE TISSUE BOX COVER

(Shown on page 15)

Size: 6½"w x 9¼"h x 7"d
(Fits a 4¼"w x 5¼"h x 4¼"d boutique tissue box.)

Supplies: Worsted weight yarn (refer to Master Key), silver metallic yarn, four 10½" x 13½" sheets of clear 7 mesh plastic canvas, one 10½" x 13½" sheet of white 7 mesh plastic canvas, #16 tapestry needle, assorted miniature silk flowers and greenery, and craft glue

Stitches Used: French Knot, Gobelin Stitch, Mosaic Stitch, Overcast Stitch, and Tent Stitch

Instructions: Follow charts to cut Fence pieces from white plastic canvas. Cut remaining pieces from clear plastic canvas. Stitch Lawn through both thicknesses of plastic canvas. Stitch remaining pieces. Complete background of Front, Side, and Back pieces with blue Tent Stitches as indicated on charts. Match symbols and use Overcast Stitches to join pieces together as instructed below.

Using white yarn, join one Window Box Front piece to one Side #1 piece. Join Front to Side #2. Join Bottom to Front and Sides. Repeat for remaining Window Box pieces to make four Window Boxes. Matching ♦'s and ✿'s, tack Window Boxes to Tissue Box Cover Front, Back, and Side pieces.

Using matching color yarn, join Chimney Front to Chimney Sides. Join Chimney Back to Chimney Sides. Using tan yarn, join Roof pieces together between ♠'s. Matching ✳'s, join unworked edges of Chimney to Roof using blue yarn.

Using matching color yarn, join Front to Sides. Join Back to Sides. Using white yarn, join Roof to Front. Join Roof to Back. Glue Roof to Sides.

Matching ★'s and ■'s, join Front, Back, and Sides to Lawn through three thicknesses of plastic canvas using yarn color to match house.

Matching ♥'s, join Front Fence pieces to Lawn through three thicknesses of plastic canvas using lt green yarn. Matching ✕'s, join Side Fence pieces to Lawn. Matching ▲'s, join Back Fence pieces to Lawn. Using white yarn, join Front Fence pieces to Side Fence pieces. Join Side Fence pieces to Back Fence. Using lt green yarn, join Lawn together in front of door.

Glue flowers in Window Boxes. Glue Roof Trim pieces to Front and Back.

Design by Peggy Astle.

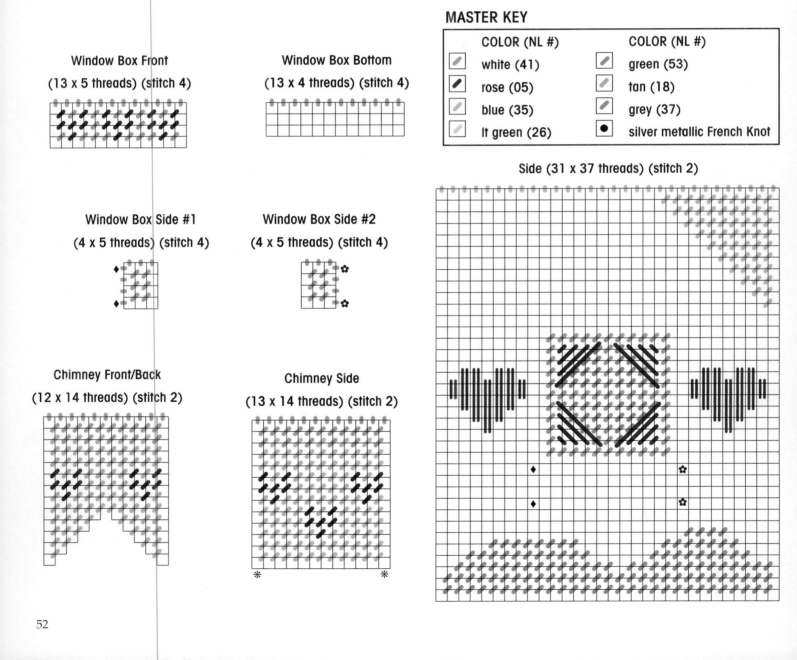

Window Box Front
(13 x 5 threads) (stitch 4)

Window Box Bottom
(13 x 4 threads) (stitch 4)

Window Box Side #1
(4 x 5 threads) (stitch 4)

Window Box Side #2
(4 x 5 threads) (stitch 4)

Chimney Front/Back
(12 x 14 threads) (stitch 2)

Chimney Side
(13 x 14 threads) (stitch 2)

Side (31 x 37 threads) (stitch 2)

MASTER KEY

	COLOR (NL #)		COLOR (NL #)
	white (41)		green (53)
	rose (05)		tan (18)
	blue (35)		grey (37)
	lt green (26)	●	silver metallic French Knot

Roof (31 x 25 threads) (stitch 2)

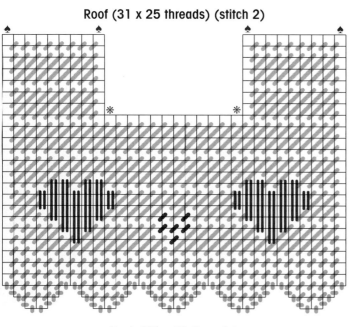

Roof Trim (24 x 24 threads) (stitch 2)

Back (31 x 51 threads)

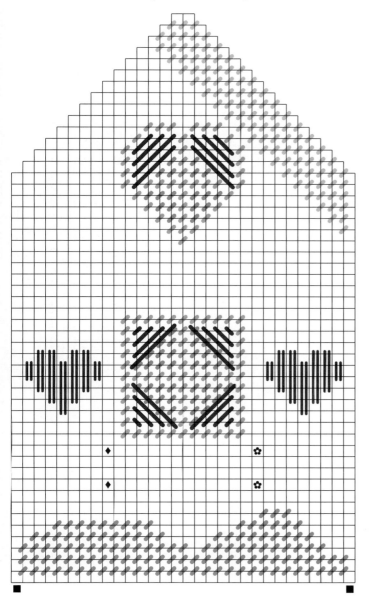

Front (31 x 51 threads)

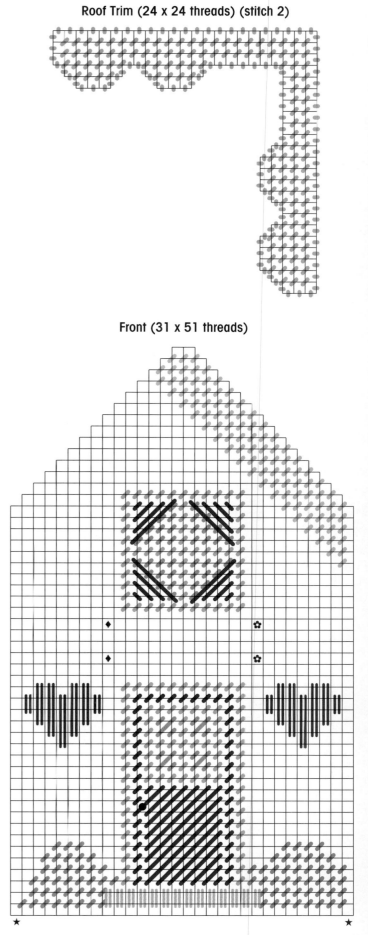

Continued on page 54

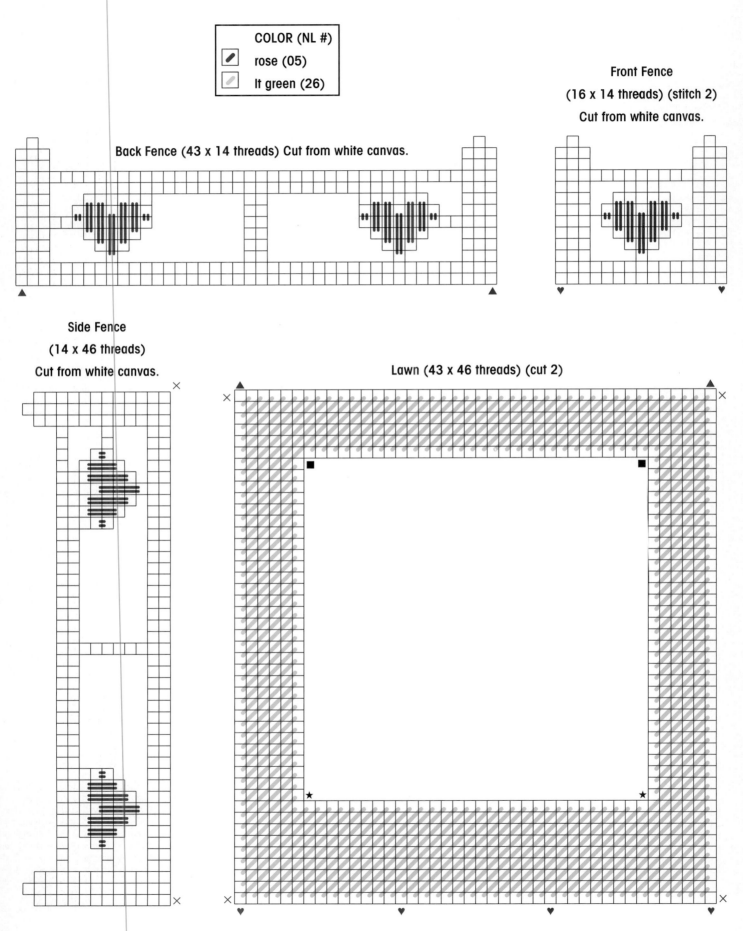

COLOR (NL #)

✎ rose (05)

◸ lt green (26)

Front Fence
(16 x 14 threads) (stitch 2)
Cut from white canvas.

Back Fence (43 x 14 threads) Cut from white canvas.

Side Fence
(14 x 46 threads)
Cut from white canvas.

Lawn (43 x 46 threads) (cut 2)

FLORAL FRAME

(Shown on page 16)

Size: 8"w x 10"h
(Photo opening is 4¼"w x 6"h.)

Supplies: Worsted weight yarn, two 10½" x 13½" sheets of clear 7 mesh stiff plastic canvas, and #16 tapestry needle

Stitches Used: French Knot, Gobelin Stitch, Overcast Stitch, and Tent Stitch

Instructions: Follow chart to cut and stitch Front. Complete background of Front with white Tent Stitches as indicated on chart. Cut a piece of plastic canvas 54 x 66 threads for Back. Cut a piece of plastic canvas 16 x 66 threads for Stand Top. Cut a piece of plastic canvas 16 x 16 threads for Stand Bottom. Back, Stand Top, and Stand Bottom are not stitched.

Refer to Diagram to construct Frame. Using rose yarn, join Stand Top to Stand Bottom along one short edge. Tack Stand to Back. Join Front to Back along unworked edges of Front. Cover unworked edge of Back.

Design by Ann Townsend.

COLOR (NL #)	
⬜	white (41)
⬜	rose (05)
⬜	blue (35)
⬜	green (53)
⦿	green (53) French Knot

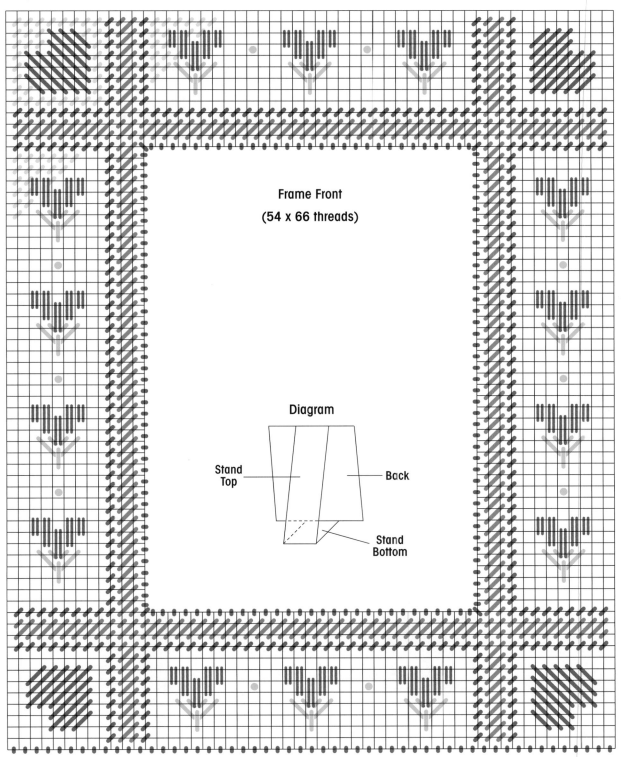

Frame Front
(54 x 66 threads)

Diagram

Stand Top — Back
Stand Bottom

VICTORIAN DOILY

(Shown on page 16)

Size: 11¹/₂"w x 11¹/₂"h

Supplies: Worsted weight yarn, four Uniek® 6" heart shapes, #16 tapestry needle, cork or felt (optional), and craft glue (optional)

Stitches Used: Cross Stitch, Gobelin Stitch, Mosaic Stitch, Overcast Stitch, and Tent Stitch

Instructions: Follow chart to stitch pieces. Using blue yarn, join Sections together between ✳'s. Cover unworked edges of Doily. If desired, cut cork or felt slightly smaller than stitched piece and glue to wrong side of Doily.

Design by Ann Townsend.

"WELCOME FRIEND" DOOR HANGER

(Shown on page 17)

Size: 3¹/₄"w x 9¹/₂"h

Supplies: Worsted weight yarn, one 10¹/₂" x 13¹/₂" sheet of clear 7 mesh plastic canvas, and #16 tapestry needle

Stitches Used: Backstitch, Gobelin Stitch, Overcast Stitch, and Tent Stitch

Instructions: Follow chart to cut and stitch design. Refer to photo for yarn color and cover unworked edges of Door Hanger.

Design by Rosalie Dettloff.

	COLOR (NL #)
	white (41)
	rose (05)
	blue (35)
	green (53)

Door Hanger

(21 x 64 threads)

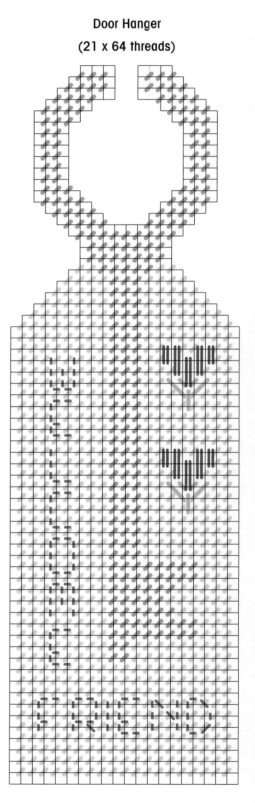

Doily Section

(stitch 4)

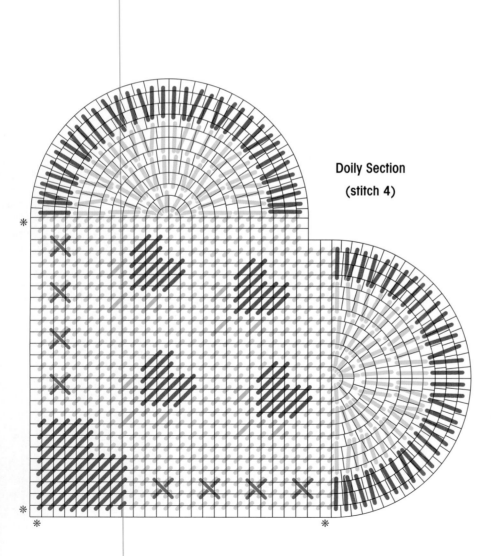

56

FLORAL SACHET CUBES

(Shown on page 17)

Size: 2" cube

Supplies for One Cube: Worsted weight yarn, one 10¹/₂" x 13¹/₂" sheet of clear 7 mesh plastic canvas, #16 tapestry needle, and potpourri

Stitches Used: Cross Stitch, French Knot, Gobelin Stitch, Overcast Stitch, and Tent Stitch

Instructions: Follow chart to cut and stitch pieces to make desired Cube. Using blue yarn, join five sides together. Fill Cube with potpourri. Join remaining side to Cube.

Designs by Ann Townsend.

VICTORIAN FLOWERPOT COVER

(Shown on page 17)

Size: 5"h x 7" dia.

Supplies: Worsted weight yarn, one 13¹/₂" x 22" sheet of clear 7 mesh plastic canvas, #16 tapestry needle, and 5"h x 6" dia. planter

Stitches Used: Gobelin Stitch, Overcast Stitch, and Tent Stitch

Instructions: Cut a 142 x 34 thread piece of plastic canvas. Follow chart to stitch design, repeating stitch patterns to right edge of canvas. Complete background with white Tent Stitches as shown on chart. Using matching color yarn, join short edges of canvas together to form a cylinder.

Design by Ann Townsend.

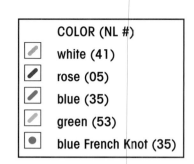

COLOR (NL #)	
✎	white (41)
✎	rose (05)
✎	blue (35)
✎	green (53)
●	blue French Knot (35)

Sachet Cube #1

(13 x 13 threads) (stitch 6)

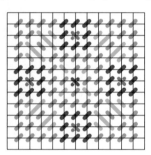

Sachet Cube #2

(13 x 13 threads) (stitch 6)

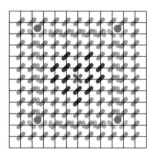

Sachet Cube #3

(13 x 13 threads) (stitch 6)

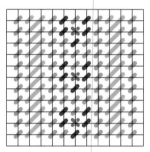

Flowerpot Cover (142 x 34 threads)

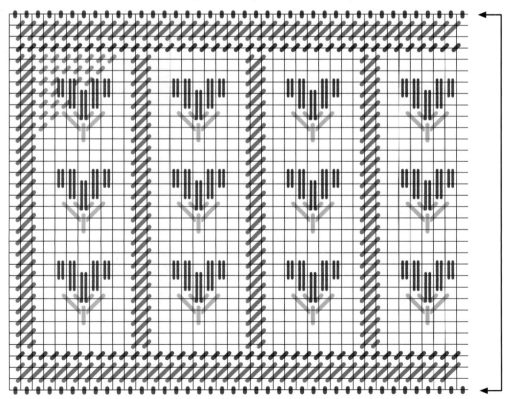

Continue stitching design to right edge of canvas

Home Is Where The Heart Can Rest

BED COASTER SET

(Shown on page 18)

Bed Size: 4"w x 4¹⁄₂"h x 5³⁄₄"d
Coaster Size: 3¹⁄₄"w x 4³⁄₄"h
Supplies: Worsted weight yarn, three 10¹⁄₂" x 13¹⁄₂" sheets of clear 7 mesh plastic canvas, one 10¹⁄₂" x 13¹⁄₂" sheet of almond 7 mesh plastic canvas, #16 tapestry needle, 12" length of 1³⁄₈"w ecru pregathered fabric ruffle, cork or felt (optional), and craft glue
Stitches Used: French Knot, Gobelin Stitch, Mosaic Stitch, Overcast Stitch, Smyrna Cross Stitch, and Tent Stitch
Instructions: Follow charts to cut and stitch pieces. If desired, cut a piece of cork or felt slightly smaller than each Coaster. Glue cork or felt to back of Coasters.

Using dk brown yarn, join Headboard pieces together. Join Footboard pieces together.

Using matching color yarn, join long edges of Quilt Top to Quilt Side pieces.

For Bed, cut two pieces of almond plastic canvas 34 x 15 threads each for Sides. Cut two pieces of almond plastic canvas 24 x 15 threads each for Ends. Cut a piece of almond plastic canvas 24 x 34 threads for Bottom. Side, End, and Bottom pieces are not stitched. Using ecru yarn, join Sides and Ends together, alternating long and short pieces to form a rectangle. Join Bottom to Sides and Ends. If desired, cover unworked edges with ecru yarn.

Glue fabric ruffle to Sides of Bed. Place Quilt on top of Bed for placement and glue Quilt to Headboard and Footboard.

Bed design by Susan Albert and Susan Lizotte.
Coaster #1 and #2 designs by Joan Green.

QUILT MUG INSERT

(Shown on page 21)

Size: 3¹⁄₂"h x 3" dia.
Supplies: Worsted weight yarn, one 10¹⁄₂" x 13¹⁄₂" sheet of clear 7 mesh plastic canvas, #16 tapestry needle, and parchment Crafter's Pride® Mugs-Your-Way™
Stitches Used: Gobelin Stitch, Overcast Stitch, Smyrna Cross Stitch, and Tent Stitch
Instructions: Follow chart to cut and stitch Mug Insert. Using red yarn, join ends together to form a cylinder.

Design by Joan Green.

✎ ecru		✎ lt brown	
✎ dk red		✎ brown	
✎ lt blue		✎ dk brown	
✎ blue		● dk blue French Knot	
✎ dk blue			

Coaster #1 (22 x 32 threads) (stitch 2)

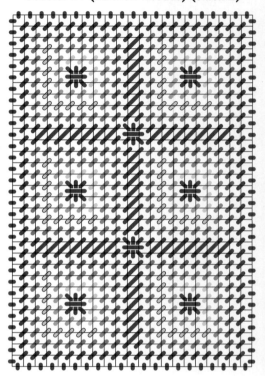

Coaster #2 (22 x 32 threads) (stitch 2)

Coaster #3 (22 x 32 threads) (stitch 2)

Quilt Top (36 x 26 threads)

Headboard (27 x 30 threads) (stitch 2)

Footboard (27 x 24 threads) (stitch 2)

Quilt Side (36 x 13 threads) (stitch 2)

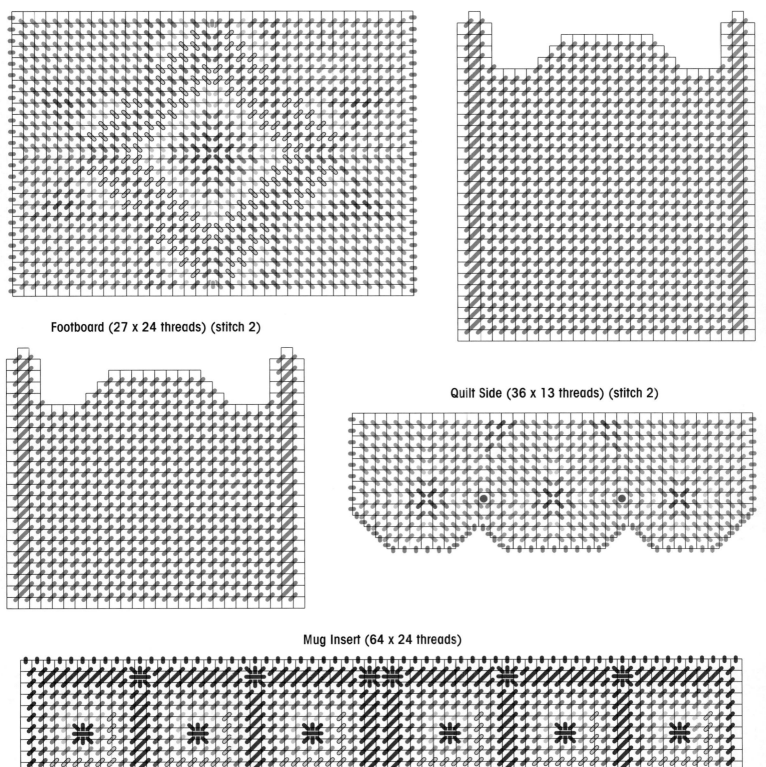

Mug Insert (64 x 24 threads)

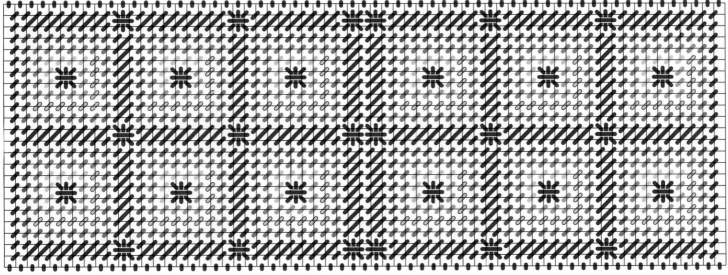

QUILT JEWELRY BOX

(Shown on page 20)

Size: 5"w x 1¹/₄"h x 3¹/₄"d

Supplies: Worsted weight yarn, one 10¹/₂" x 13¹/₂" sheet of clear 7 mesh plastic canvas, and #16 tapestry needle

Stitches Used: Gobelin Stitch, Overcast Stitch, Smyrna Cross Stitch, and Tent Stitch

Instructions: Follow charts to cut and stitch pieces. Cut a 32 x 22 thread piece of plastic canvas for Bottom. Bottom is not stitched.

Use dk blue yarn for all joining and to cover unworked edges of pieces. Join Hinge #1 to Top between ✳'s. Join Hinge #2 to Top between ■'s. Join one short edge of one Tray piece to remaining unworked edge of Hinge #1. Repeat to join remaining Tray piece to Hinge #2. If desired, cover unworked edges of Tray pieces.

Join short edges of Side pieces together, alternating Long and Short Sides to form a rectangle. Join Sides to Bottom.

Join unworked edge of Top to one Long Side. Cover unworked edge of remaining Long Side.

Box design by Eleanor Albano.
Box Top design by Joan Green.

QUILT SAMPLER

(Shown on page 19)

Size: 10¹/₄"w x 13¹/₄"h

Supplies: Worsted weight yarn, one 10¹/₂" x 13¹/₂" sheet of clear 7 mesh plastic canvas, #16 tapestry needle, sawtooth hanger, and craft glue

Stitches Used: Alternating Scotch Stitch, Backstitch, Gobelin Stitch, Overcast Stitch, Scotch Stitch, and Tent Stitch

Instructions: Follow chart to cut and stitch design. Glue sawtooth hanger to back of Sampler.

Design by Eileen Somers.

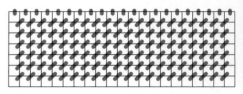

	ecru		dk blue
	dk red		lt brown
	lt blue		brown
	blue		

Short Side (22 x 8 threads) (stitch 2)

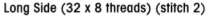

Long Side (32 x 8 threads) (stitch 2)

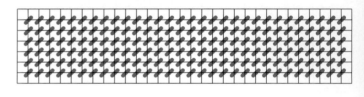

Hinge #1
(5 x 18 threads)

Tray (27 x 18 threads) (cut 2)

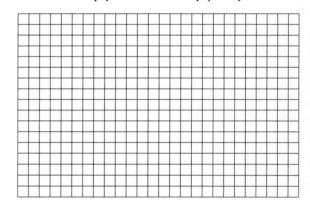

Hinge #2
(4 x 18 threads)

Top (32 x 22 threads)

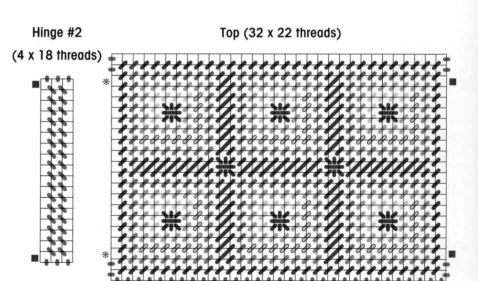

Diagram

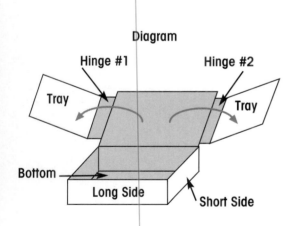

Hinge #1   Hinge #2
Tray   Tray
Bottom
Long Side   Short Side

Tray pieces hold your earrings.

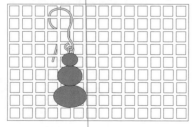

60

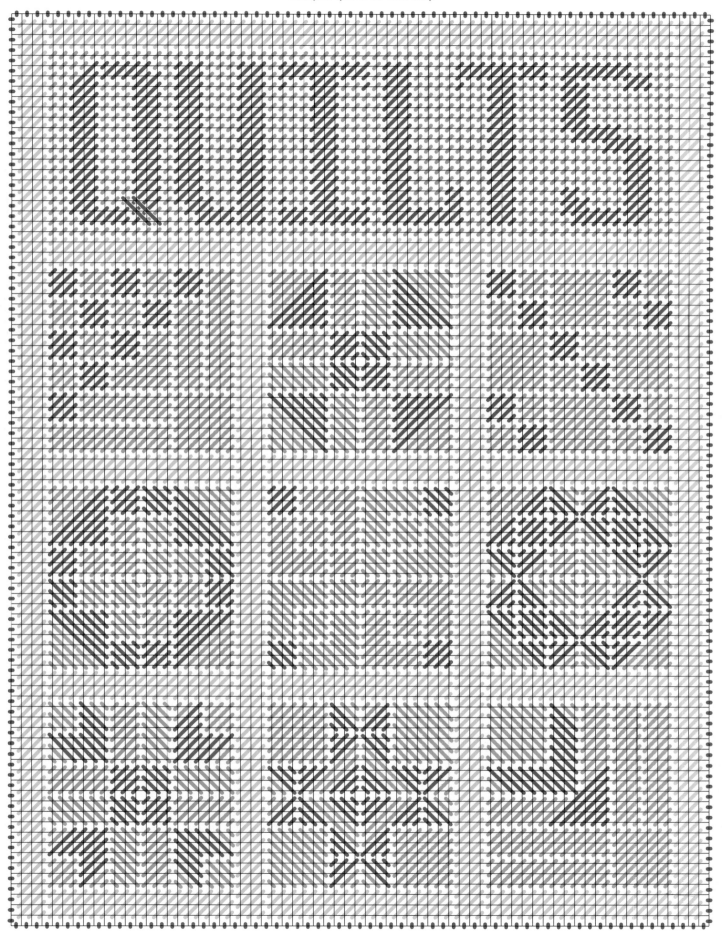

SMALL QUILT BOX

(Shown on page 21)

Size: 3¼"w x 6¼"h x 3¼"d

Supplies: Worsted weight yarn, one 10½" x 13½" sheet of clear 7 mesh plastic canvas, and #16 tapestry needle

Stitches Used: Gobelin Stitch, Overcast Stitch, and Tent Stitch

Instructions: Follow charts to cut and stitch pieces. Cut a 22 x 22 thread piece of plastic canvas for Bottom. Bottom is not stitched. Using dk red yarn, join Side pieces together to form a box. Join Bottom to Sides. Tack ends of Box Handle to back of Box Sides.

QUILT BATH BASKET

(Shown on page 20)

Size: 8¾"h x 7" dia.

Supplies: Worsted weight yarn, one 13½" x 22" sheet of clear 7 mesh plastic canvas, Darice® 9½" dia. plastic canvas circle, and #16 tapestry needle

Stitches Used: Alternating Scotch Stitch, Gobelin Stitch, Overcast Stitch, Scotch Stitch, and Tent Stitch

Instructions: Follow chart to cut and stitch Basket Handle. Cut a 22 x 146 thread piece of plastic canvas for Basket Side. Beginning at left edge of canvas, stitch Basket Side pattern twice. For Bottom, trim eight threads from circle. Bottom is not stitched.

Using lt blue yarn, join short edges of Basket Side together to form a cylinder. Join Basket Side to Bottom. Tack ends of Basket Handle to back of Basket Side.

Designs by Eileen Somers.

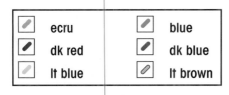

	ecru		blue
	dk red		dk blue
	lt blue		lt brown

Box Side

(22 x 22 threads) (stitch 4)

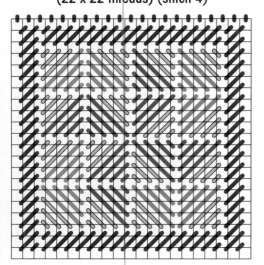

Box Handle

(5 x 57 threads)

Basket Side

(22 x 146 threads)

Basket Handle

(8 x 101 threads)

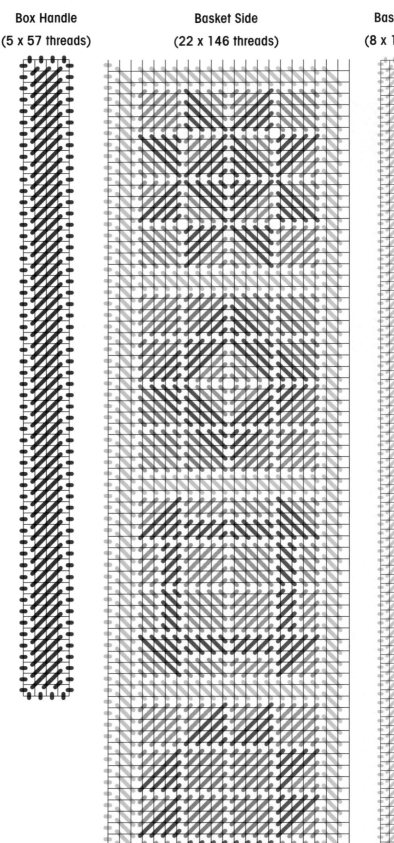

PATTERNED TISSUE BOX COVER

(Shown on page 21)

Size: 9³/₄"w x 3³/₄"h x 5"d
(Fits a 9¹/₂"w x 3¹/₄"h x 4⁵/₈"d standard tissue box.)

Supplies: Worsted weight yarn, two 10¹/₂" x 13¹/₂" sheets of almond 7 mesh plastic canvas, and #16 tapestry needle

Stitches Used: Alternating Scotch Stitch, Backstitch, Gobelin Stitch, Overcast Stitch, Scotch Stitch, and Tent Stitch

Instructions: Follow charts to cut and stitch pieces. Using dk red yarn, join short edges of Front to Sides. Join Sides to Back. Join Top to Front, Back, and Sides.

Design by LuvLee Designs.

✎	dk red

Side (34 x 25 threads) (stitch 2)

Front/Back (65 x 25 threads) (stitch 2)

Top (65 x 34 threads)

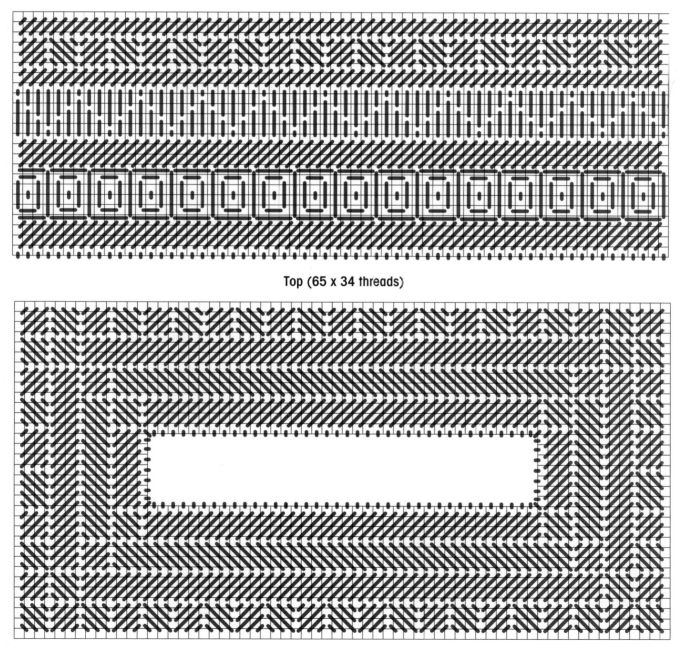

God Bless Our Country Home

BEEHIVE

(Shown on page 22)

Size: 5"w x 6"h x 5"d

Supplies: Worsted weight yarn, two 10½" x 13½" sheets of clear 7 mesh plastic canvas, #16 tapestry needle, 12" length of jute, potpourri, silk flowers, artificial berries, bees, and craft glue

Stitches Used: Gobelin Stitch, Overcast Stitch, and Tent Stitch

Instructions: Follow charts to cut and stitch pieces. Using gold yarn, join Side pieces together between ▲'s and ■'s. Tie ends of jute into a knot; glue ends inside opening on top of Beehive. Join Front to Sides. Join Bottom to Front and Sides. Glue bees, berries, and flowers to Beehive. Fill Beehive with potpourri.

Design by Robin Howard-Will.

Bottom (34 x 34 threads)

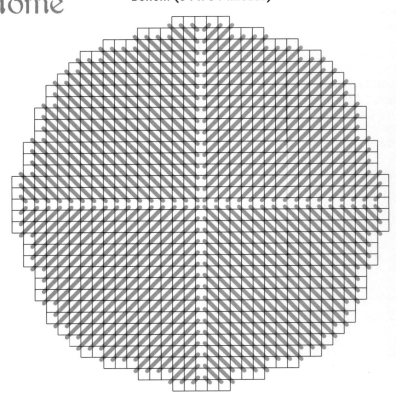

	COLOR (NL #)
⟋	gold (17)

Front (22 x 39 threads)

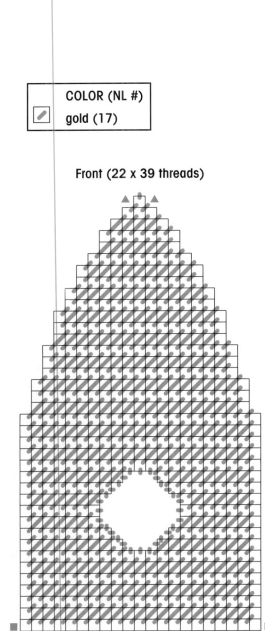

Side (22 x 39 threads) (stitch 4)

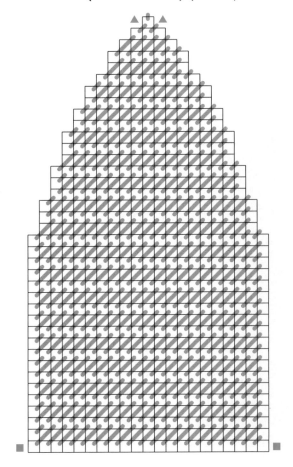

FARM MAGNETS

(Shown on page 24)

Approx. Size: 2¼"w x 3¾"h each

Supplies: Worsted weight yarn, silver metallic cord, one 10½" x 13½" sheet of clear 7 mesh plastic canvas, #16 tapestry needle, magnetic strip, and craft glue

Stitches Used: Backstitch, French Knot, Gobelin Stitch, Mosaic Stitch, Overcast Stitch, Tent Stitch, and Turkey Loop Stitch

Instructions: Follow charts to cut and stitch Farmer Front, Feed Sack, Cow (charts on page 66), and Pig pieces. Refer to photo for yarn color and cover unworked edges of stitched pieces. Glue magnetic strip to back of Magnets.

Designs by Peggy Astle.

FARMYARD DESK ORGANIZER

(Shown on page 23)

Size: 11¾"w x 8½"h x 6¼"d
(Fits a 4¼"w x 5¼"h x 4¼"d boutique tissue box.)

Supplies: Worsted weight yarn (refer to Master Key), silver metallic cord, five 10½" x 13½" sheets of clear 7 mesh plastic canvas, one 10½" x 13½" sheet of white 7 mesh plastic canvas, one 4½" dia. plastic canvas circle, #16 tapestry needle, ½" silver cow bell, 12" length of ⅛"w red ribbon, and craft glue

Stitches Used: Backstitch, Cross Stitch, French Knot, Gobelin Stitch, Mosaic Stitch, Overcast Stitch, Scotch Stitch, Tent Stitch, and Turkey Loop Stitch

Instructions: Follow charts to cut Fence pieces from white plastic canvas. Cut and stitch remaining pieces from clear plastic canvas, leaving stitches in shaded areas unworked. Refer to chart to cut Silo Bottom from plastic canvas circle along blue cutting line. Stitch Barnyard through both thicknesses of plastic canvas. Using matching color yarn, cover unworked edges of Pig, Cat, Cow, and Feed Sack. Match symbols and use Overcast Stitches to join pieces together following instructions below.

Using white yarn, join long edges of Back Pocket to Back Pocket Sides. Using blue yarn, join unworked long edges of Back Pocket Sides to pink shaded threads on Back. Using white yarn, join Back Pocket Bottom to Back Pocket, Back Pocket Sides, and Back.

Work stitches in green shaded area to join Back to Side B between ◆'s. Work stitches in pink shaded area to join Front to Side B between ✳'s. Work stitches in blue shaded area to join Sloping Roof to Side B between ♠'s. Using white yarn, join Side C to Front and Back between ▼'s.

Cut a 31 x 16 thread piece of clear plastic canvas for Bottom. Bottom is not stitched. Using green yarn, join Bottom to Side C, Front, Back, and Side B.

Work stitches in blue shaded area to join Left and Right Shutters to unworked threads in loft on Side A. Using white yarn, join Side A to Front between ♣'s. Join one short edge of one Fence A piece to Front and Side A through three thicknesses of plastic canvas. Join Side A to Back between ❖'s. Join one short edge of remaining Fence A piece to Back and Side A through three thicknesses of plastic canvas. Join short

edges of Fence B to Fence A pieces. Using green yarn, join Barnyard to Side A and Fence through all thicknesses of plastic canvas.

Using white yarn, join Right Roof #1 to Left Roof #1 along unworked edges between ▲'s and ■'s. Join Right Roof #1 to Right Roof #2 between ✖'s. Join Left Roof #1 to Left Roof #2 between ★'s.

Using white yarn, join Right Roof #2 to Side B between ✿'s. Join Left Roof #2 to Side A between ♥'s. Join Roof to Front and Back.

Using grey yarn, join Milk Can Front to Sides. Join Back to Sides. Join Rim pieces to Front, Back, and Sides. Join Bottom to Front, Back, and Sides. Glue Milk Can to Back Pocket.

Refer to photo for yarn color and join Farmer Front to Farmer Back. Tack Farmer to Barnyard. Glue Pig, Cat, Cow, and Feed Sack to Desk Organizer.

For Cow's tail, cut two 6" lengths of white yarn and one 6" length of black yarn. Tie one end of yarn pieces into a knot ½" from ends; trim ends. Braid yarn and tie a knot ½" from remaining ends; fringe ends. Glue tail to Cow.

Using blue yarn, join long edges of Silo together to form a cylinder. Using green yarn, join Silo Side to Bottom along remaining unworked edge of Side. Using matching color yarn, join ends of Silo Roof together between ✿'s and ✚'s. Using grey yarn, fold and join inside edges of Silo Roof together as indicated by arrows.

Design by Peggy Astle.

MASTER KEY

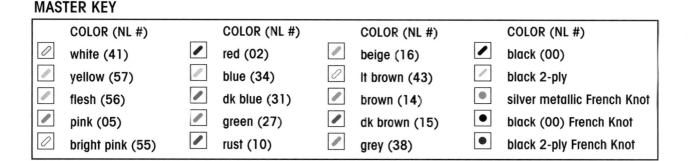

	COLOR (NL #)		COLOR (NL #)		COLOR (NL #)		COLOR (NL #)
	white (41)		red (02)		beige (16)		black (00)
	yellow (57)		blue (34)		lt brown (43)		black 2-ply
	flesh (56)		dk blue (31)		brown (14)		silver metallic French Knot
	pink (05)		green (27)		dk brown (15)		black (00) French Knot
	bright pink (55)		rust (10)		grey (38)		black 2-ply French Knot

Pig
(12 x 12 threads)

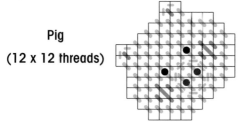

Cat
(7 x 7 threads)

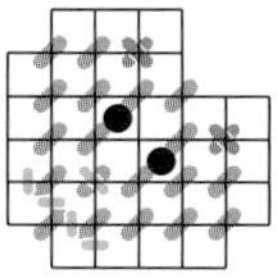

Continued on page 66

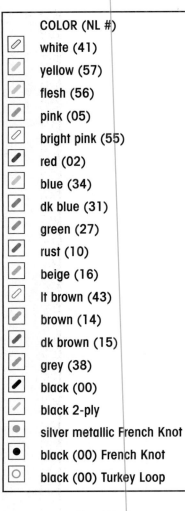

COLOR (NL #)

- white (41)
- yellow (57)
- flesh (56)
- pink (05)
- bright pink (55)
- red (02)
- blue (34)
- dk blue (31)
- green (27)
- rust (10)
- beige (16)
- lt brown (43)
- brown (14)
- dk brown (15)
- grey (38)
- black (00)
- black 2-ply
- silver metallic French Knot
- black (00) French Knot
- black (00) Turkey Loop

Farmer Front
(18 x 32 threads)

Farmer Back
(18 x 32 threads)

Feed Sack
(12 x 14 threads)

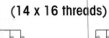

Front
(46 x 49 threads)

Cow
(14 x 16 threads)

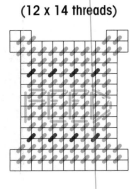
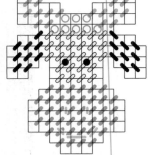

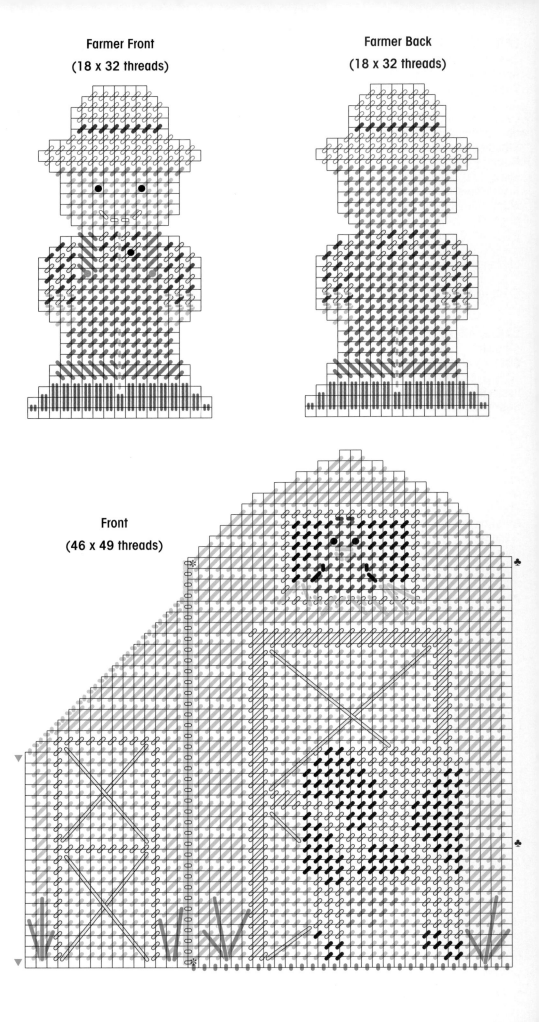

Milk Can Front/Back

(8 x 9 threads)

(stitch 2)

Milk Can Side

(4 x 7 threads)

(stitch 2)

Side B (31 x 39 threads)

Milk Can Rim

(4 x 4 threads)

(stitch 2)

Milk Can Bottom

(4 x 8 threads)

Back (46 x 49 threads)

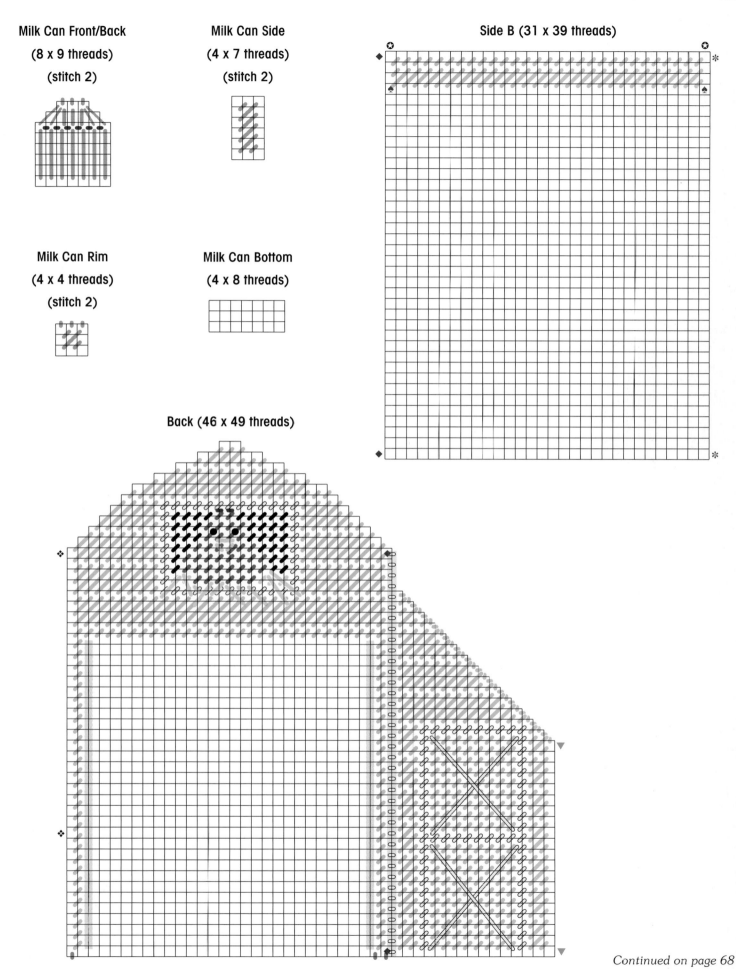

Continued on page 68

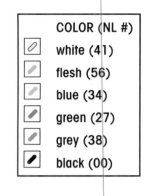

COLOR (NL #)

- white (41)
- flesh (56)
- blue (34)
- green (27)
- grey (38)
- black (00)

Barnyard

(32 x 31 threads) (cut 2)

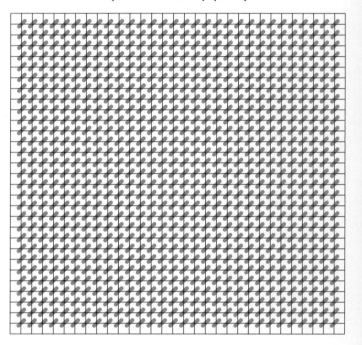

Side C (31 x 21 threads)

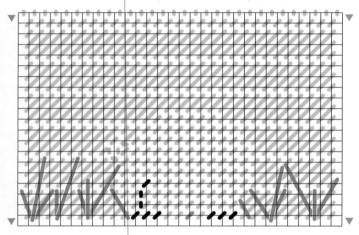

Fence A (32 x 12 threads)

Cut 2 from white canvas.

Fence B (31 x 12 threads)

Cut 1 from white canvas.

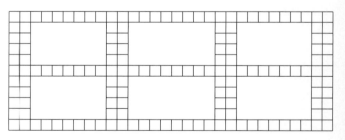

Back Pocket Side
(5 x 30 threads)
(stitch 2)

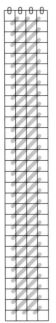

Back Pocket Bottom
(5 x 27 threads)

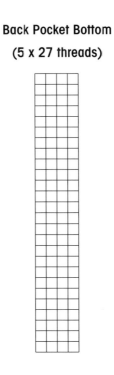

Back Pocket
(27 x 30 threads)

Left Roof #1 (31 x 11 threads)

Left Roof #2 (31 x 10 threads)

Right Roof #1 (31 x 11 threads)

Right Roof #2 (31 x 10 threads)

Sloping Roof (31 x 23 threads)

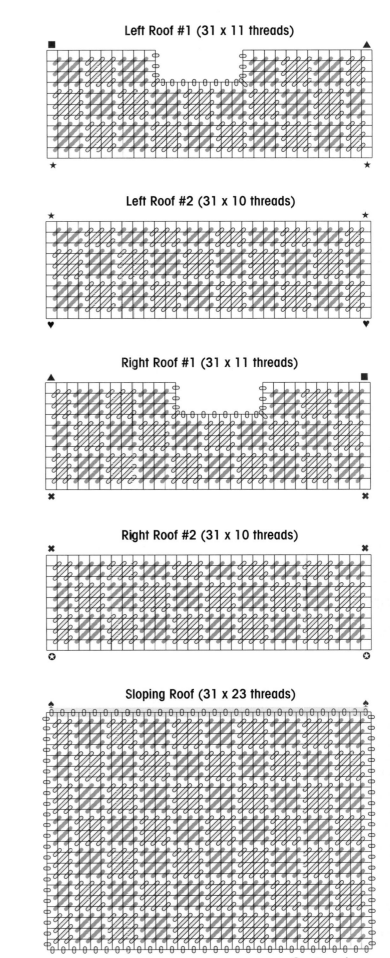

Continued on page 70

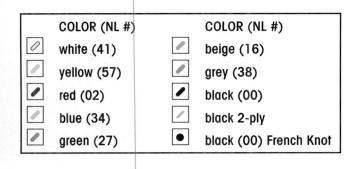

COLOR (NL #)		COLOR (NL #)	
⬦	white (41)	⬦	beige (16)
⬦	yellow (57)	⬦	grey (38)
⬦	red (02)	⬦	black (00)
⬦	blue (34)	⬦	black 2-ply
⬦	green (27)	●	black (00) French Knot

Silo Bottom

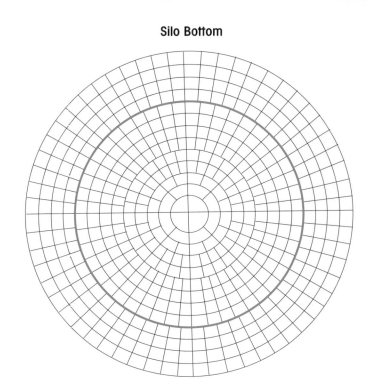

Silo Side (69 x 50 threads)

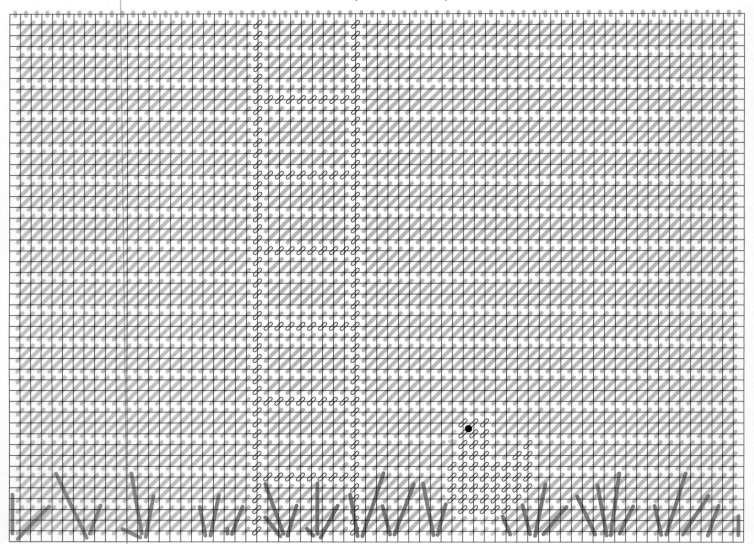

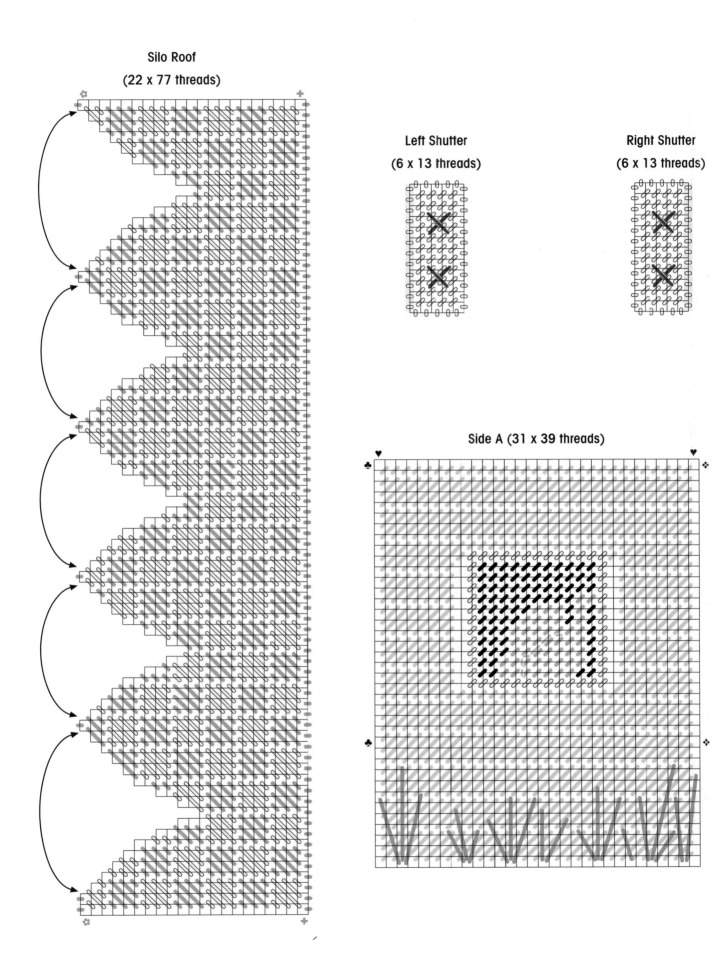

Silo Roof
(22 x 77 threads)

Left Shutter
(6 x 13 threads)

Right Shutter
(6 x 13 threads)

Side A (31 x 39 threads)

BARN

(Shown on page 24)

Size: 4"w x 2³/₄"h x 3¹/₂"d

Supplies: Worsted weight yarn, one 10¹/₂" x 13¹/₂" sheet of clear 7 mesh plastic canvas, #16 tapestry needle, and craft glue

Stitches Used: Gobelin Stitch, Overcast Stitch, and Tent Stitch

Instructions: Follow charts to cut and stitch pieces, leaving stitches in shaded areas unworked.

Work stitches in blue shaded area to join one Roof B piece to one Upper Side between ■'s and ✲'s. Repeat for remaining Roof B and Upper Side pieces.

Matching ▲'s and ★'s, work stitches in yellow shaded areas to join Front and Back to one Upper Side. Repeat for remaining Upper Side.

Matching ♥'s and ✛'s, join Front and Back to one Lower Side using red yarn. Repeat for remaining Lower Side.

Using white yarn, join unworked edge of Loft Door to upper opening of Front. Join Left and Right Door pieces to lower openings of Front.

Cut a 24 x 20 thread piece of plastic canvas for Bottom. Bottom is not stitched. Using red yarn, join Barn to Bottom. Cover unworked edges of Bottom.

Using white yarn, join Roof A pieces together along unworked edges. Glue Roof A to Barn. Glue Roof B pieces to Barn.

Design by Terry A. Ricioli.

"KISS THE COOK" JAR LID

(Shown on page 25)

Size: 2⁵/₈" dia.

Supplies: Worsted weight yarn, one 10¹/₂" x 13¹/₂" sheet of clear 7 mesh plastic canvas, regular jar lid ring (2¹/₄" dia. opening), #16 tapestry needle, and craft glue

Stitches Used: Backstitch, Cross Stitch, and Tent Stitch

Instructions: Follow chart to cut and stitch design. Glue stitched piece to jar lid ring.

Design by Anne Van Wagner Childs.

CURLY TAILED PIG JAR LID

(Shown on page 25)

Size: 3¹/₄" dia.

Supplies: Worsted weight yarn, one 10¹/₂" x 13¹/₂" sheet of clear 7 mesh plastic canvas, wide-mouth jar lid ring (3" dia. opening), #16 tapestry needle, and craft glue

Stitches Used: Backstitch, Gobelin Stitch, and Tent Stitch

Instructions: Follow chart to cut and stitch design, working Tent Stitches over completed Gobelin Stitches. Tie a 12" length of blue yarn into a bow and trim ends. Glue bow to pig. Glue stitched piece to jar lid ring.

Design by Anne Van Wagner Childs.

HONEYCOMB JAR LID

(Shown on page 25)

Size: 3¹/₄" dia.

Supplies: Worsted weight yarn, one 10¹/₂" x 13¹/₂" sheet of clear 7 mesh plastic canvas, wide-mouth jar lid ring (3" dia. opening), #16 tapestry needle, and craft glue

Stitches Used: Backstitch, Gobelin Stitch, Overcast Stitch, and Tent Stitch

Instructions: Follow charts to cut and stitch pieces. Glue Honeycomb to jar lid ring. Glue Bees to Honeycomb and jar lid ring.

Design by Karen Plank.

"FRESH EGGS" SIGN

(Shown on page 25)

Size: 10"w x 7¹/₄"h

Supplies: Worsted weight yarn, two 10¹/₂" x 13¹/₂" sheets of clear 7 mesh plastic canvas, #16 tapestry needle, poster board, ¹/₃ yd of fabric, paper-backed fusible web, sawtooth hanger, and craft glue

Stitches Used: Backstitch, Gobelin Stitch, Overcast Stitch, and Tent Stitch

Instructions: Follow charts to cut and stitch Front, "e" center, and "g" center pieces. For Back, cut a Front piece, omitting openings. Back is not stitched.

Trim poster board and fabric to ¹/₄" smaller on all sides than Front. Follow manufacturer's instructions to apply fusible web to back of fabric. Fuse fabric to poster board. Place poster board between Front and Back.

Using red yarn, join Front to Back. Glue "e" center and "g" center pieces to Sign. Glue sawtooth hanger to Back.

Design by MizFitz.

Barn Lower Side

(20 x 3 threads) (stitch 2)

Barn Front (24 x 17 threads)

Barn Back (24 x 17 threads)

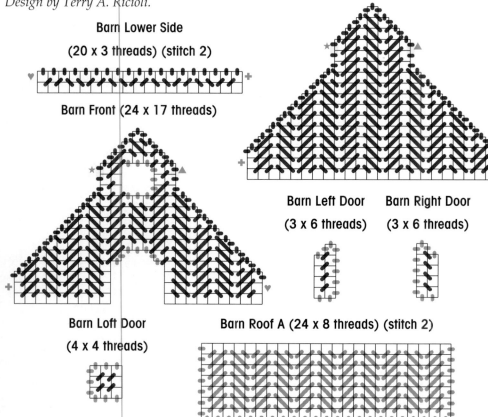

Barn Left Door   **Barn Right Door**

(3 x 6 threads)   **(3 x 6 threads)**

Barn Loft Door

(4 x 4 threads)

Barn Roof A (24 x 8 threads) (stitch 2)

Barn Upper Side

(20 x 3 threads) (stitch 2)

Barn Roof B

(24 x 14 threads) (stitch 2)

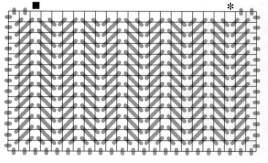

COLOR (NL #)

white (41)	blue (33)
yellow (57)	brown 2-ply
flesh (56)	black (00)
red (02)	black 2-ply

Bee
(8 x 7 threads) (stitch 2)

Honeycomb Jar Lid
(22 x 22 threads)

Curly Tailed Pig Jar Lid
(22 x 22 threads)

"Kiss The Cook" Jar Lid
(18 x 18 threads)

"Fresh Eggs" Sign Front (66 x 48 threads)

Home Away From Home

MOTOR HOME TISSUE BOX COVER

(Shown on pages 26 and 28)

Size: 7½"w x 4¾"h x 4¾"d
(Fits a 4¼"w x 5¼"h x 4¼"d boutique tissue box.)

Supplies: Worsted weight yarn, embroidery floss, silver metallic yarn, two 10½" x 13½" sheets of clear 7 mesh plastic canvas, five 3" dia. plastic canvas circles, #16 tapestry needle, and craft glue.

Stitches Used: Backstitch, Cross Stitch, Gobelin Stitch, Overcast Stitch, and Tent Stitch

Instructions: Follow charts to cut and stitch pieces. Refer to chart to cut Wheels from circles along blue cutting line. Cut a 31 x 31 thread piece of plastic canvas for Center Brace. Cut a 31 x 14 thread piece of plastic canvas for Bottom. Center Brace and Bottom are not stitched. Match symbols and use Overcast Stitches to join pieces together as follows.

Using yarn color to match Back, join Side #1 to Back between ★'s and ✕'s. Join Side #2 to Back between ■'s and ♥'s.

Using matching color yarn, join Top to Back between ■'s and ★'s. Using white yarn, join Side #1 to Top between ★'s and ●'s. Join Side #2 to Top between ✳'s and ■'s.

Using white yarn, join Top to Windshield and one short edge of Center Brace through three thicknesses of plastic canvas between ●'s and ✳'s.

Using white yarn, join Windshield to Front between ▲'s and ♦'s. Referring to photo for yarn color, join Front to Side #1 between ▲'s and ✿'s. Join Front to Side #2 between ♦'s and ✚'s.

Using white yarn, join Windshield to Side #1 between ●'s and ▲'s. Join Windshield to Side #2 between ✳'s and ♦'s.

Using blue yarn, join remaining unworked edge of Front to one long edge of Bottom. Join unworked edge of Side #1 to one short edge of Bottom. Join unworked edge of Side #2 to remaining short edge of Bottom. Join remaining long edge of Bottom to Center Brace.

Glue Wheels to Motor Home Tissue Box Cover.

Design by Peggy Astle.

Top (31 x 38 threads)

Back (31 x 31 threads)

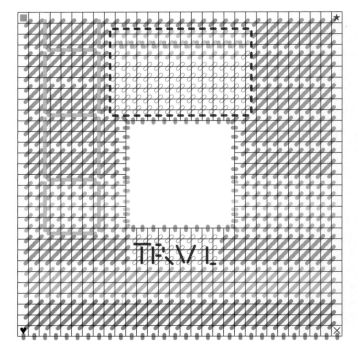

Front (31 x 19 threads)

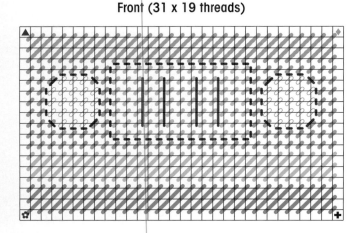

Windshield (31 x 18 threads)

Wheel
(stitch 5)

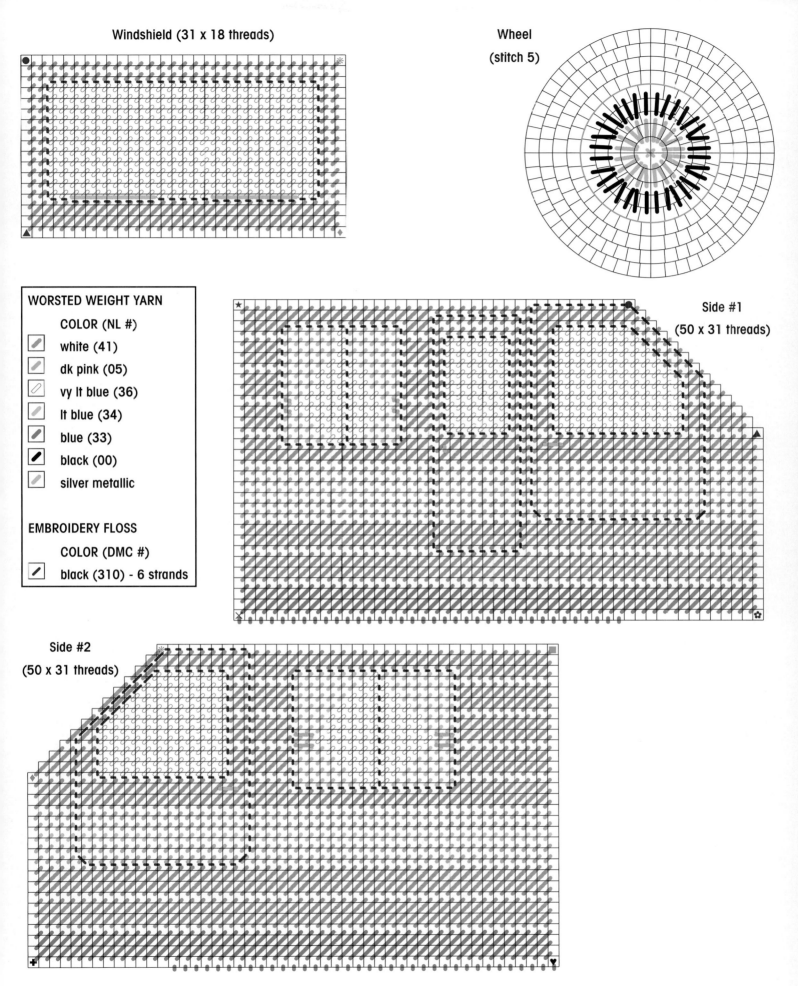

WORSTED WEIGHT YARN

COLOR (NL #)

	white (41)
	dk pink (05)
	vy lt blue (36)
	lt blue (34)
	blue (33)
	black (00)
	silver metallic

EMBROIDERY FLOSS

COLOR (DMC #)

	black (310) - 6 strands

Side #1
(50 x 31 threads)

Side #2
(50 x 31 threads)

DIMENSIONAL FISH

(Shown on page 27)

Size: 5"w x 15¾"h x 1¼"d

Supplies for One Fish: Worsted weight yarn, two 12" x 18" sheets of clear 7 mesh plastic canvas, #16 tapestry needle, polyester fiberfill, and cord or rope

Stitches Used: Backstitch, Overcast Stitch, and Tent Stitch

Instructions: Follow chart to cut and stitch Fish Front. For Back, cut a Front piece, turn piece over, and cover with vy lt blue Tent Stitches.

Using vy lt blue yarn, join Front to Back while stuffing with polyester fiberfill. Knot cord and place knotted end inside mouth of Fish before joining mouth area together.

Design by Trish Suder.

CAMPER COASTER SET

(Shown on page 28)

Holder Size: 6"w x 4¾"h x 1½"d

Coaster Size: 4½"w x 3¾"h

Supplies: Worsted weight yarn, embroidery floss, two 10½" x 13½" sheets of clear 7 mesh stiff plastic canvas, #16 tapestry needle, cork or felt (optional), and craft glue

Stitches Used: Backstitch, Gobelin Stitch, Overcast Stitch, and Tent Stitch

Instructions: Follow charts to cut and stitch pieces. Stitch Coaster Holder Bottom through both thicknesses of plastic canvas.

Using green yarn, join unworked long edge of Coaster Holder Back to Bottom through all thicknesses of plastic canvas. Join Sides to Bottom. Join Sides to Back.

Using green yarn, tack Tree #1 to Coaster Holder Back. Join Tree #3 to Bottom through all thicknesses of plastic canvas between ▲'s and ■'s. Using brown yarn, join Tree #2 to Bottom. Using green yarn, tack Tree #2 to Side #2.

If desired, cut a piece of cork or felt slightly smaller than each Coaster. Glue cork or felt to back of Coasters.

Design by Dorothy Tabor.

COLOR (NL #)	
⊘	white (41)
◢	dk pink (05)
◢	burgundy (03)
⊘	vy lt blue (36)
◢	lt blue (34)
◢	blue (33)
◢	dk blue (31)
◢	lt green (25)
◢	green (27)
◢	tan (18)
◢	brown (13)
◢	grey (38)
◢	black (00)

COLOR (DMC #)	
◢	white (blanc) - 6 strands
◢	black (310) - 6 strands

Tree #1
(18 x 17 threads)

Tree #2
(14 x 18 threads)

Tree #3
(14 x 14 threads)

Chart Note: This chart represents one 105 x 33 thread canvas piece. It is spread across two pages to make it large enough to be followed easily. No threads or stitches are repeated from one page to the next.

Fish Front
(105 x 33 threads)

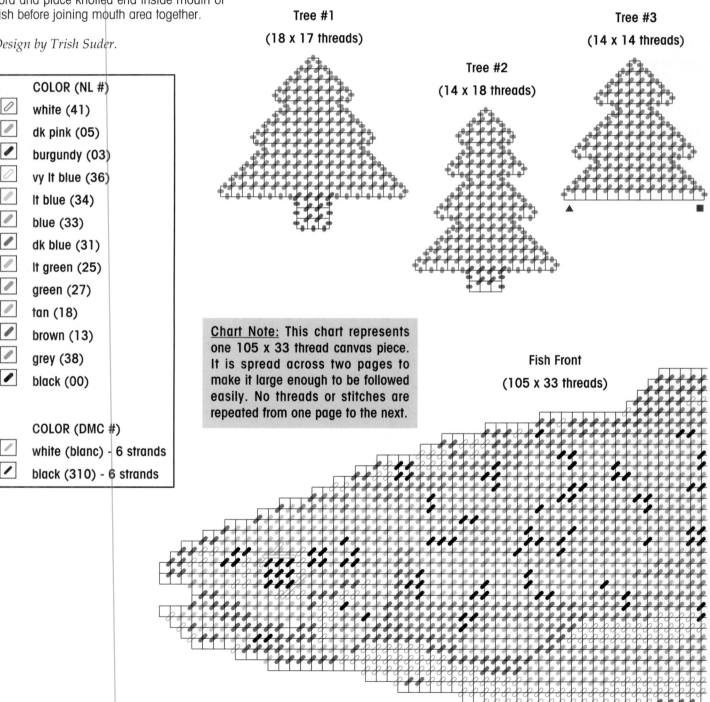

76

Coaster #1 (31 x 25 threads) (stitch 2)

Coaster Holder Back (36 x 31 threads)

Coaster #2 (31 x 25 threads) (stitch 2)

Coaster Holder Side #1
(10 x 4 threads)

Coaster Holder Side #2
(10 x 4 threads)

Coaster Holder Bottom
(10 x 36 threads)
(cut 2)

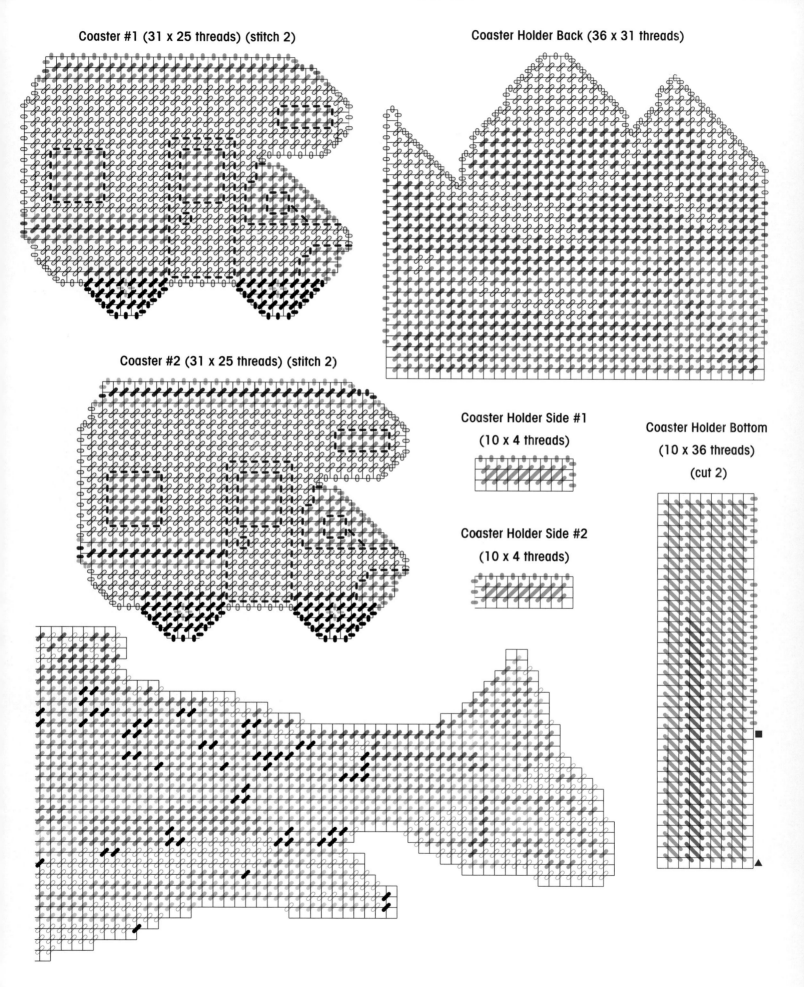

GOLF BAG PENCIL HOLDER

(Shown on page 28)

Size: 4¹/₄"w x 5¹/₂"h x 2"d

Supplies: Worsted weight yarn, one 10¹/₂" x 13¹/₂" sheet of clear 7 mesh plastic canvas, 3" dia. circle, #16 tapestry needle, three ¹/₂" white pom-poms, three pencils, and craft glue

Stitches Used: Alternating Scotch Stitch, Gobelin Stitch, Overcast Stitch, and Tent Stitch

Instructions: Follow charts to cut and stitch pieces. Refer to chart to cut Bottom from plastic canvas circle along blue cutting line. Using burgundy yarn, join Pocket Front to Sides along unworked long edges. Join Bottom to Front and Sides.

Matching ✳'s and ▲'s, tack Pocket Side #1 to Golf Bag Side using dk blue yarn. Matching ♥'s and ✖'s, tack Pocket Side #2 to Side. Matching ■'s and ●'s, tack Pocket Top to Golf Bag Side. Tack Bottom to Golf Bag Side. Using matching color yarn, join short edges of Golf Bag Side together, forming a cylinder. Using dk blue yarn, join Golf Bag Side to Bottom.

Using dk blue yarn, bend and tack Handle to Golf Bag. Join unworked edges of Pencil Top #1 together. Slide Pencil Top #1 onto one pencil. Glue one pom-pom to Pencil Top #1. Repeat for Pencil Top #2 and #3.

Design by Margaret Bauer.

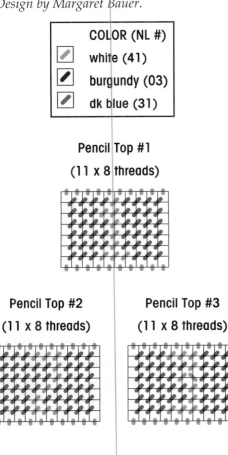

COLOR (NL #)	
	white (41)
	burgundy (03)
	dk blue (31)

Pencil Top #1

(11 x 8 threads)

Pencil Top #2

(11 x 8 threads)

Pencil Top #3

(11 x 8 threads)

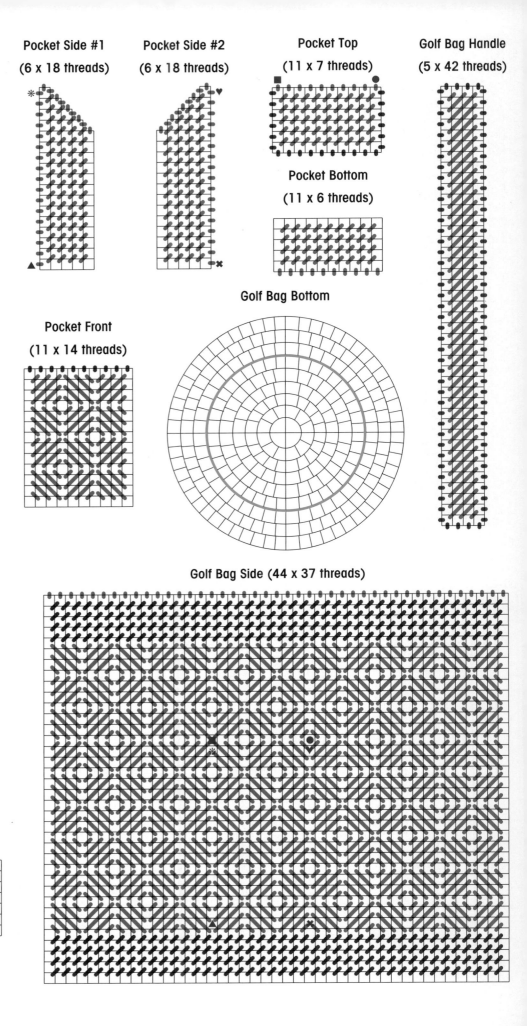

Pocket Side #1

(6 x 18 threads)

Pocket Side #2

(6 x 18 threads)

Pocket Top

(11 x 7 threads)

Golf Bag Handle

(5 x 42 threads)

Pocket Bottom

(11 x 6 threads)

Pocket Front

(11 x 14 threads)

Golf Bag Bottom

Golf Bag Side (44 x 37 threads)

CAMPER MAGNET SET

(Shown on page 29)

Approx. Size: 4¹⁄₂"w x 2¹⁄₄"h each

Supplies: Worsted weight yarn, embroidery floss, one 10¹⁄₂" x 13¹⁄₂" sheet of clear 7 mesh plastic canvas, #16 tapestry needle, ten ¹⁄₂" black buttons, magnetic strip, and craft glue

Stitches Used: Backstitch, Overcast Stitch, and Tent Stitch

Instructions: Follow charts to cut and stitch pieces. Using white yarn, tack buttons to stitched pieces. Glue Camper Shell to Truck. Glue magnetic strip to back of each Magnet.

Motor Home, Truck, and Camper designs by Millie Shelton. Sign design by Fran Way Bohler.

WORSTED WEIGHT YARN	EMBROIDERY FLOSS
COLOR (NL #)	**COLOR (DMC #)**
white (41)	dk blue (3750) - 6 strands
dk pink (05)	black (310) - 6 strands
burgundy (03)	
blue (33)	
dk blue (31)	
grey (38)	
black (00)	

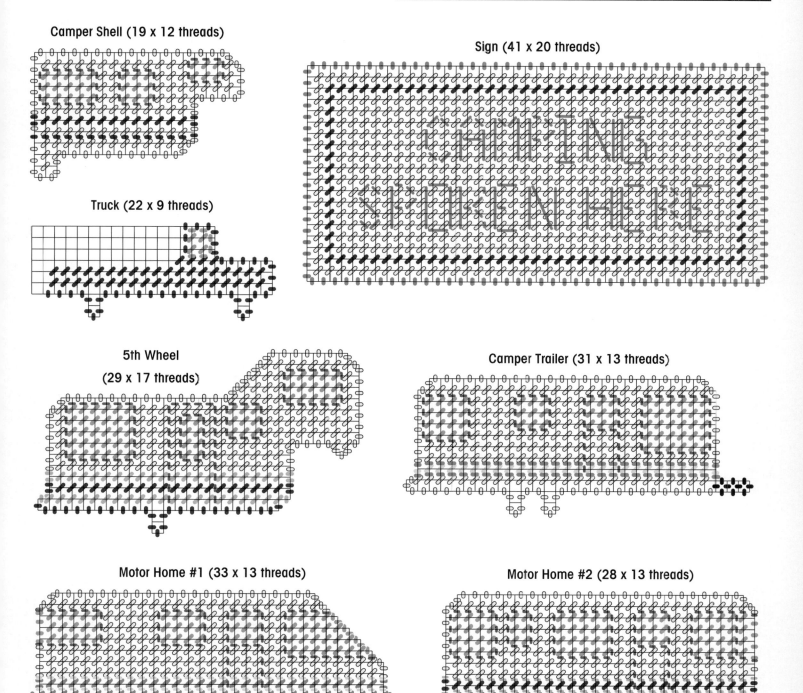

Camper Shell (19 x 12 threads)

Truck (22 x 9 threads)

Sign (41 x 20 threads)

5th Wheel (29 x 17 threads)

Camper Trailer (31 x 13 threads)

Motor Home #1 (33 x 13 threads)

Motor Home #2 (28 x 13 threads)

Happiness Is Homegrown

PRODUCE STAND TISSUE BOX COVER

(Shown on page 31)

Size: 8"w x 6³/₄"h x 7"d
(Fits a 4¹/₄"w x 5¹/₄"h x 4¹/₄"d boutique tissue box.)

Supplies: Worsted weight yarn, three 10¹/₂" x 13¹/₂" sheets of clear 7 mesh plastic canvas, and #16 tapestry needle

Stitches Used: Backstitch, Cross Stitch, French Knot, Gobelin Stitch, Mosaic Stitch, Overcast Stitch, Smyrna Cross Stitch, and Tent Stitch

Instructions: Follow charts to cut and stitch pieces, leaving shaded areas unworked. Match symbols and use Overcast Stitches to join pieces together as instructed below.

Using tan yarn, join Front Vegetable Display to pink shaded thread on Front between ■'s and ▲'s. Join Front Vegetable Display to Front Stand between ✳'s and ✕'s. Using white yarn, match ✳'s and join Front Stand to one Right Stand End piece along short edge of Front Stand. Matching ✕'s, join Front Stand to one Left Stand End piece. Using tan yarn, join Front Vegetable Display to Right Stand End between ■'s and ✳'s. Join Front Vegetable Display to Left Stand End between ✕'s and ▲'s. Repeat for Back pieces.

Using tan yarn, join one Side Vegetable Display piece to yellow shaded thread on Side #1 between ■'s and ▲'s. Join Side Vegetable Display to one Side Stand piece between ✳'s and ✕'s. Using white yarn, match ✳'s and join Side Stand to one Right Stand End piece along short edge of Side Stand. Matching ✕'s, join Side Stand to one Left Stand End piece. Using tan yarn, join Side Vegetable Display to Right Stand End between ■'s and ✳'s. Join Side Vegetable Display to Left Stand End between ✕'s and ▲'s. Repeat for Side #2 pieces.

Using white yarn, join Front to Side #1 between ▼'s and ★'s. Join Front to Side #2 between ◆'s and ✚'s. Join Back to Sides. Join Front to Side #1 and Stand End pieces through four thicknesses of plastic canvas from ★'s to ✿'s. Join Front to Side #2 and Stand End pieces from ✚'s to ✿'s. Join Back to Sides and Stand Ends.

Using green yarn, join one long edge of Awning Top to Awning Front. Join remaining long edge of Awning Top to Awning Back. Referring to photo for yarn colors used, join Awning to Front, Back, and Sides.

Using white yarn, tack one Sign piece to Awning Front between ♥'s. Repeat to tack remaining Sign piece to Awning Back.

Design by Dick Martin.

Front/Back

(38 x 32 threads) (stitch 2)

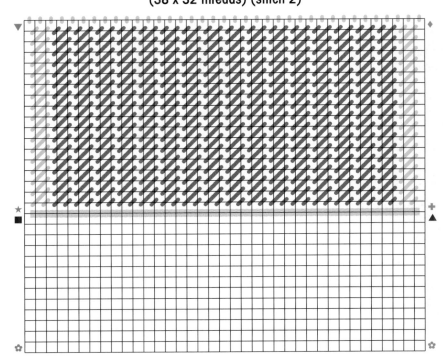

Front/Back Vegetable Display

(38 x 8 threads) (stitch 2)

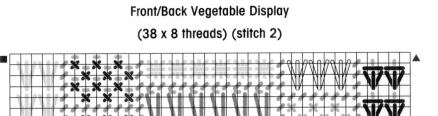

Front/Back Stand

(38 x 11 threads) (stitch 2)

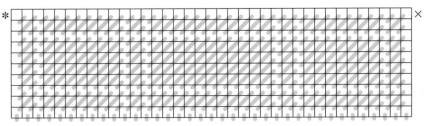

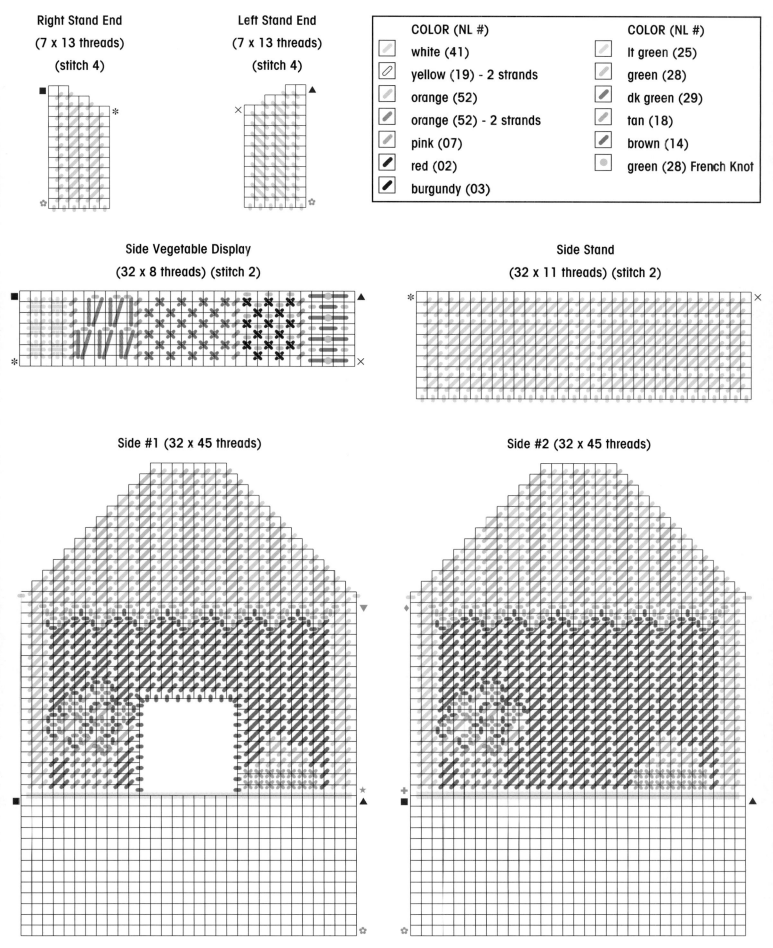

Right Stand End

(7 x 13 threads)

(stitch 4)

Left Stand End

(7 x 13 threads)

(stitch 4)

	COLOR (NL #)			COLOR (NL #)
	white (41)			lt green (25)
	yellow (19) - 2 strands			green (28)
	orange (52)			dk green (29)
	orange (52) - 2 strands			tan (18)
	pink (07)			brown (14)
	red (02)			green (28) French Knot
	burgundy (03)			

Side Vegetable Display

(32 x 8 threads) (stitch 2)

Side Stand

(32 x 11 threads) (stitch 2)

Side #1 (32 x 45 threads)

Side #2 (32 x 45 threads)

Continued on page 82

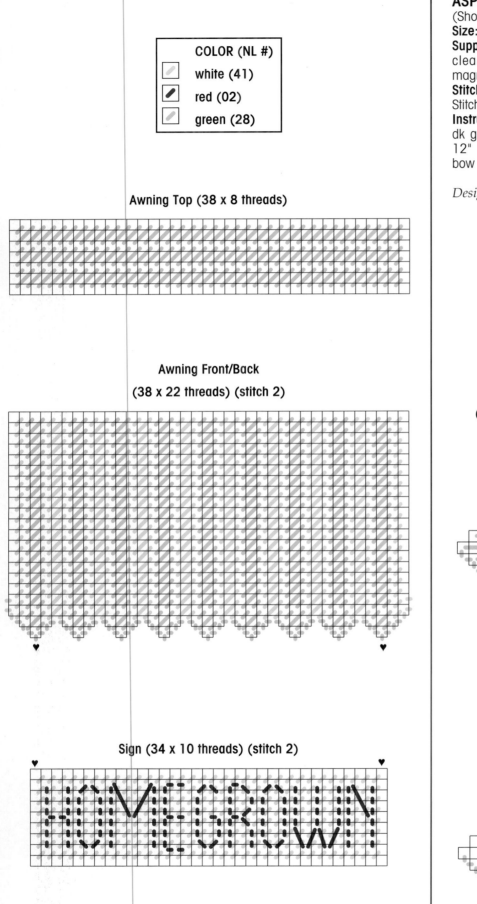

COLOR (NL #)
white (41)
red (02)
green (28)

Awning Top (38 x 8 threads)

Awning Front/Back
(38 x 22 threads) (stitch 2)

Sign (34 x 10 threads) (stitch 2)

ASPARAGUS MAGNET

(Shown on page 30)

Size: 2"w x 4"h x 1/2"d

Supplies: Worsted weight yarn, 10 1/2" x 13 1/2" sheet of clear 7 mesh plastic canvas, #16 tapestry needle, magnetic strip, and craft glue

Stitches Used: Gobelin Stitch, Overcast Stitch, and Tent Stitch

Instructions: Follow charts to cut and stitch pieces. Using dk green yarn, match ★'s and join Front to Back. Tie a 12" length of red yarn into a bow and trim ends. Glue bow to Front. Glue magnetic strip to Magnet.

Design by Dick Martin.

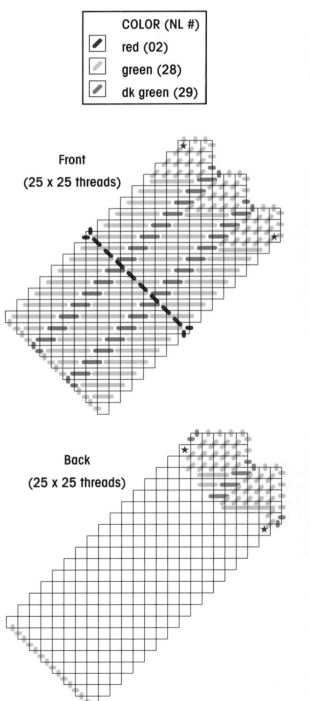

COLOR (NL #)
red (02)
green (28)
dk green (29)

Front
(25 x 25 threads)

Back
(25 x 25 threads)

PEAS MAGNET

(Shown on page 30)
Size: 1¼"w x 4"h x ½"d
Supplies: Worsted weight yarn, 10½" x 13½" sheet of clear 7 mesh plastic canvas, #16 tapestry needle, magnetic strip, and craft glue
Stitches Used: Backstitch, Gobelin Stitch, Overcast Stitch, Smyrna Cross Stitch, and Tent Stitch

Instructions: Follow charts to cut and stitch pieces. Matching ♥'s, tack Peas to Back at arrows using lt green yarn. Using green yarn, join Right Side to Back between ■'s. Join Left Side to Back between ★'s. Join top and bottom of Right Side to Left Side along unworked edges. Glue magnetic strip to Magnet.

Design by Dick Martin.

COLOR (NL #)	
	lt green (25)
	lt green (25) - 2 strands
	green (28)
	dk green (29)

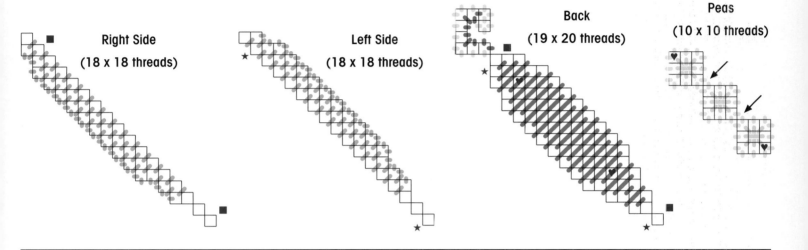

Right Side (18 x 18 threads)

Left Side (18 x 18 threads)

Back (19 x 20 threads)

Peas (10 x 10 threads)

CAULIFLOWER MAGNET

(Shown on page 30)
Size: 3¼"w x 2¾"h x ½"d
Supplies: Worsted weight yarn, 10½" x 13½" sheet of clear 7 mesh plastic canvas, #16 tapestry needle, magnetic strip, and craft glue
Stitches Used: French Knot, Overcast Stitch, and Tent Stitch

Instructions: Follow charts to cut pieces. For Front and Back, work Overcast Stitches, then French Knots. Stitch Leaves and remaining stitches on Back. Matching ★'s, tack Front to Back using white yarn. Using green yarn, join Leaves to Back between ■'s. Glue magnetic strip to Magnet.

Design by Dick Martin.

COLOR (NL #)	
	white (41)
	lt green (25)
	green (28)
	white (41) French Knot

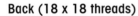

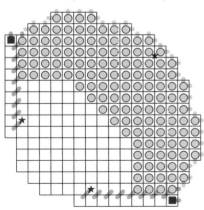

Back (18 x 18 threads)

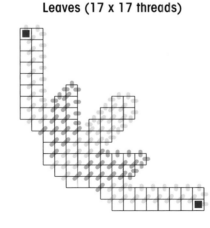

Leaves (17 x 17 threads)

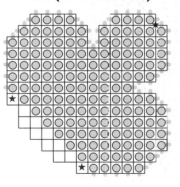

Front (15 x 15 threads)

East-West, Home Is Best

ADOBE VILLAGE
(Shown on page 32)

Size: $11\frac{1}{2}$"w x 6"h x $5\frac{1}{2}$"d

Supplies: Worsted weight yarn (refer to Master Key), four $10\frac{1}{2}$" x $13\frac{1}{2}$" sheets of clear 7 mesh plastic canvas, #16 tapestry needle, and craft glue

Stitches Used: Backstitch, French Knot, Gobelin Stitch, Overcast Stitch, Scotch Stitch, and Tent Stitch

Instructions: Follow charts to cut and stitch pieces, leaving shaded areas unstitched. Using dk green yarn, join Cactus #8 pieces together. Using matching color yarn, cover unworked edges of all Cactus, Pot, and Ladder pieces.

Matching ▲'s and ●'s, refer to Diagram and join Unit #1 Top to #1 Front using tan yarn. Matching ♥'s and ✖'s, join Unit #1 to Unit #2 Top along blue shaded area. Matching ✳'s and ■'s, join Unit #2 Top to #2 Front using rose yarn. Matching ♠'s and ♦'s, join Units #1 and 2 to Large Unit Front along yellow shaded area using matching color yarn.

Matching ★'s and ❖'s, join Unit #3 Top to #3 Front using lt brown yarn. Matching ♥'s and ❄'s, join #3 Top to #3 Back. Matching ▼'s, join Unit #3 to pink shaded area on Large Unit Top.

Matching ☞'s and ✿'s, join Large Unit Top to Large Unit Front using blue yarn. Join remaining unworked long edge of Large Unit Top to Large Unit Back.

Matching ✚'s and ◗'s, join Unit #4 Top to #4 Front using lt green yarn. Join remaining unworked long edge of #4 Top to #4 Back. Join Unit #4 to Large Unit along green shaded area.

Matching ✕'s and ✪'s, join Unit #5 Top to #5 Front using lt green yarn. Join remaining unworked long edge of #5 Top to #5 Back.

Matching ✳'s and ■'s, join Units to Bottom using matching color yarn. Glue Unit #5 to Large Unit Top.

For Snake, bend canvas into three loops starting $\frac{1}{4}$" from head and tack in place using grey yarn. Glue a $\frac{1}{2}$" length of red yarn to wrong side of Snake's head for tongue. Glue Snake, Cactus, Pot, and Ladder pieces to Adobe Village.

Design by Becky Dill.

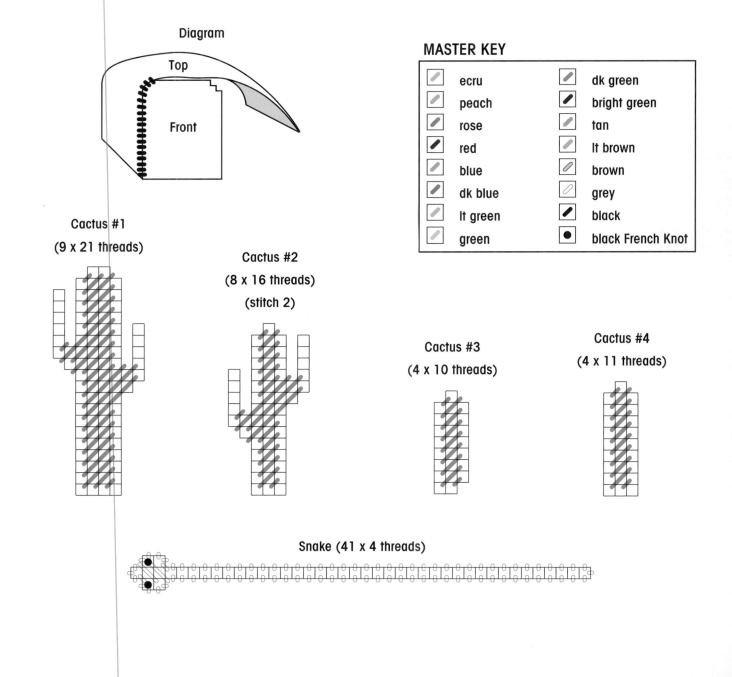

Diagram

Top

Front

MASTER KEY

✎	ecru	✎	dk green
✎	peach	✎	bright green
✎	rose	✎	tan
✎	red	✎	lt brown
✎	blue	✎	brown
✎	dk blue	✎	grey
✎	lt green	✎	black
✎	green	●	black French Knot

Cactus #1
(9 x 21 threads)

Cactus #2
(8 x 16 threads)
(stitch 2)

Cactus #3
(4 x 10 threads)

Cactus #4
(4 x 11 threads)

Snake (41 x 4 threads)

Large Unit Front (41 x 30 threads)

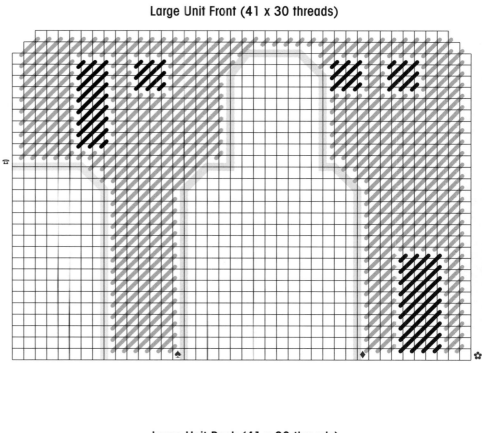

Large Unit Back (41 x 30 threads)

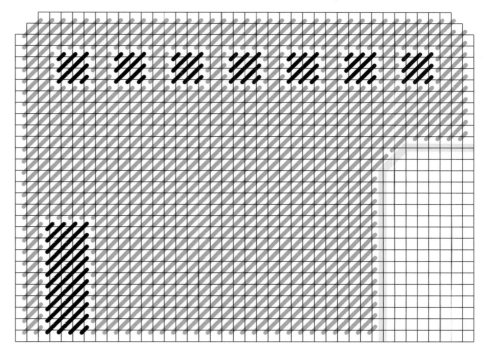

Continued on page 86

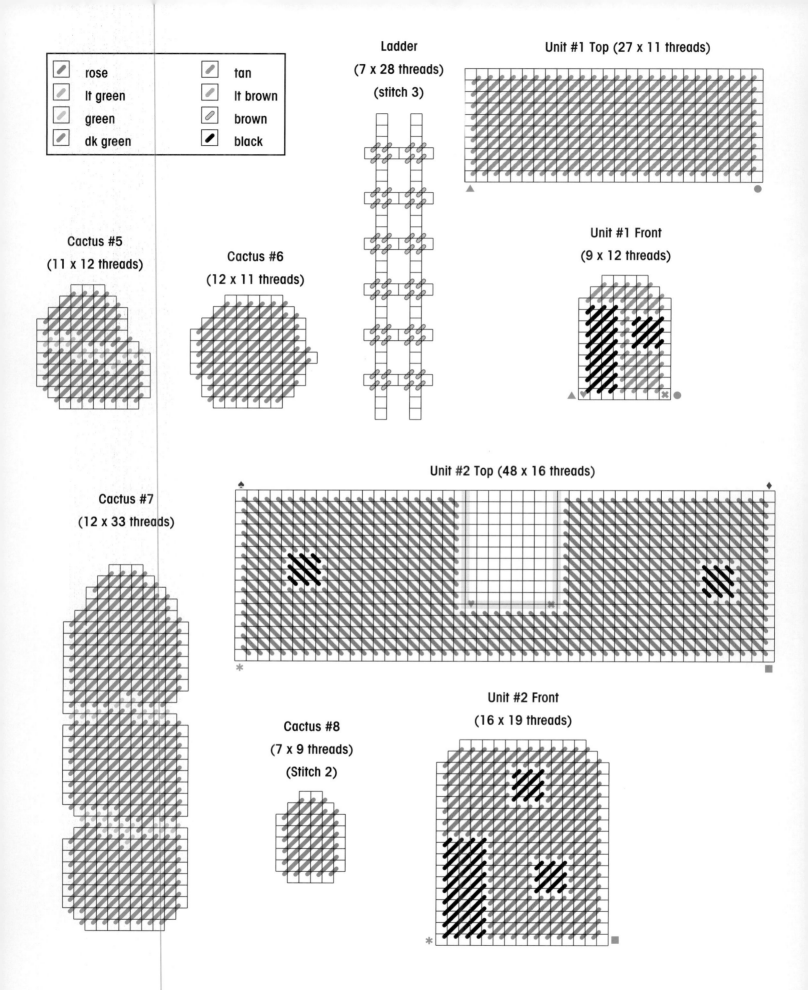

rose

lt green

green

dk green

tan

lt brown

brown

black

Cactus #5
(11 x 12 threads)

Cactus #6
(12 x 11 threads)

Ladder
(7 x 28 threads)
(stitch 3)

Unit #1 Top (27 x 11 threads)

Unit #1 Front
(9 x 12 threads)

Cactus #7
(12 x 33 threads)

Unit #2 Top (48 x 16 threads)

Cactus #8
(7 x 9 threads)
(Stitch 2)

Unit #2 Front
(16 x 19 threads)

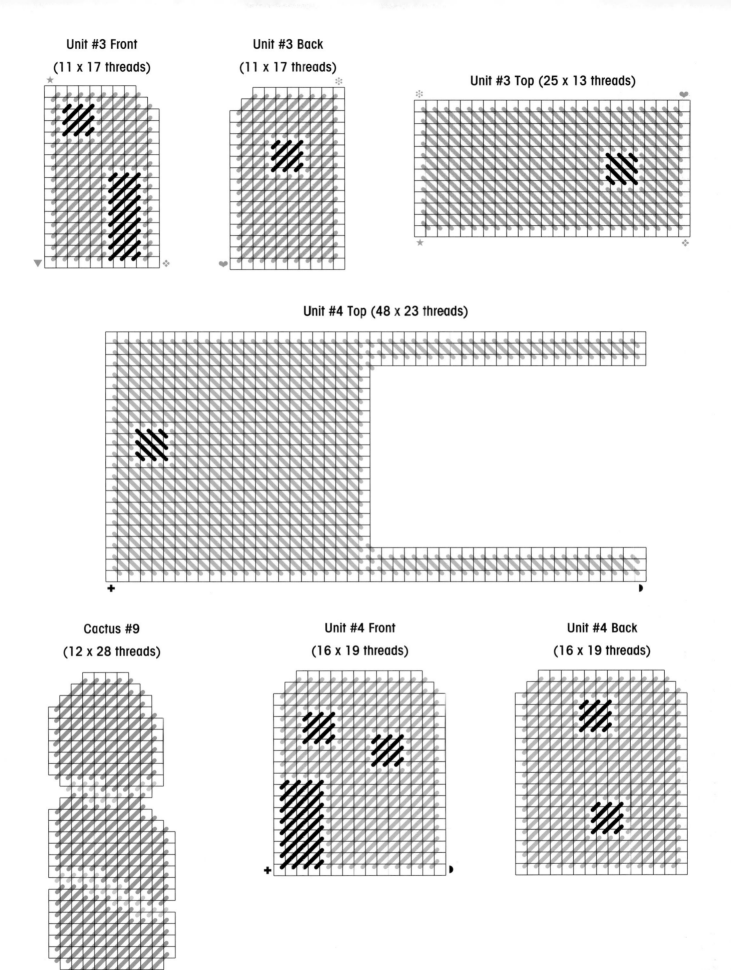

Unit #3 Front
(11 x 17 threads)

Unit #3 Back
(11 x 17 threads)

Unit #3 Top (25 x 13 threads)

Unit #4 Top (48 x 23 threads)

Cactus #9
(12 x 28 threads)

Unit #4 Front
(16 x 19 threads)

Unit #4 Back
(16 x 19 threads)

Continued on page 88

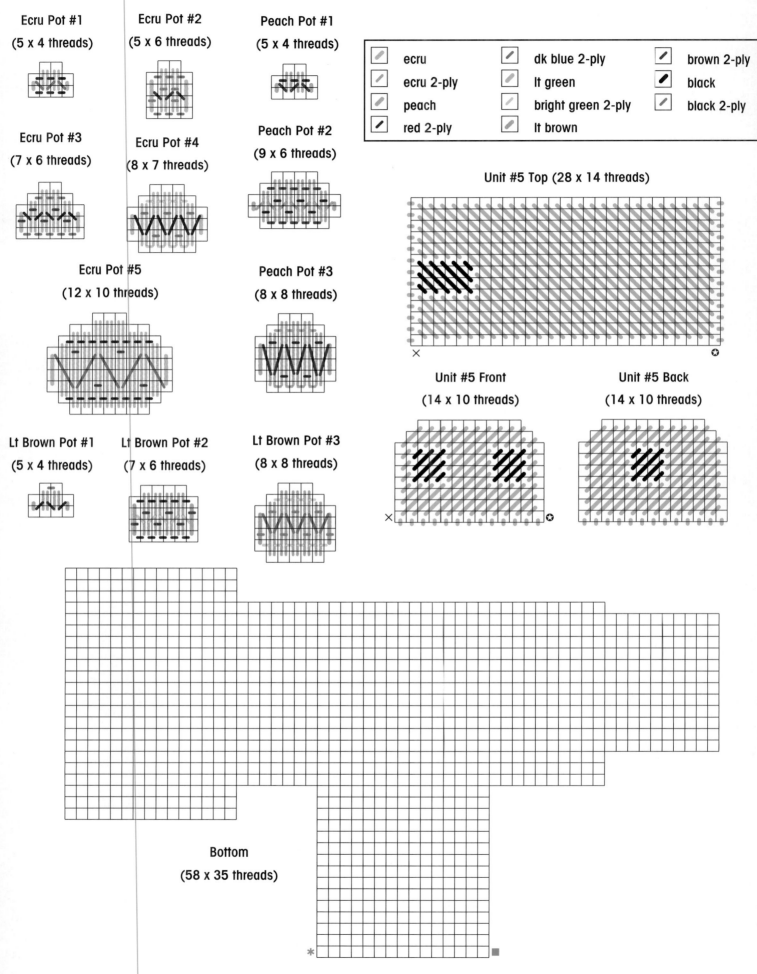

Ecru Pot #1
(5 x 4 threads)

Ecru Pot #2
(5 x 6 threads)

Peach Pot #1
(5 x 4 threads)

Ecru Pot #3
(7 x 6 threads)

Ecru Pot #4
(8 x 7 threads)

Peach Pot #2
(9 x 6 threads)

Ecru Pot #5
(12 x 10 threads)

Peach Pot #3
(8 x 8 threads)

Lt Brown Pot #1
(5 x 4 threads)

Lt Brown Pot #2
(7 x 6 threads)

Lt Brown Pot #3
(8 x 8 threads)

ecru
ecru 2-ply
peach
red 2-ply

dk blue 2-ply
lt green
bright green 2-ply
lt brown

brown 2-ply
black
black 2-ply

Unit #5 Top (28 x 14 threads)

Unit #5 Front
(14 x 10 threads)

Unit #5 Back
(14 x 10 threads)

Bottom
(58 x 35 threads)

SOUTHWESTERN FRAME

(Shown on page 33)
Size: 7³/₄"w x 9¹/₂"h
(Photo opening is 5¹/₄"w x 7¹/₄"h.)
Supplies: Worsted weight yarn, two 10¹/₂" x 13¹/₂" sheets of clear 7 mesh stiff plastic canvas, #16 tapestry needle, and 3 yds of ¹/₄" dia. cord
Stitch Used: Gobelin Stitch
Instructions: Follow chart to cut Front. Place cord over pink shaded area; trim ends. Work dk blue stitches in pink shaded area to cover cord. Repeat to work variegated stitches in blue shaded area. Work blue stitches in yellow shaded area. Work remaining long stitches. For complete coverage, work two or three Gobelin Stitches in each hole.

Cut a piece of plastic canvas 49 x 62 threads for Back. Cut a piece of plastic canvas 15 x 64 threads for Stand Top. Cut a piece of plastic canvas 15 x 30 threads for Stand Bottom. Back, Stand Top, and Stand Bottom are not stitched.

Refer to Diagram to construct Frame. Using blue yarn, join Stand Top to Stand Bottom along one short edge. Join Stand to Back. Tack Back to wrong side of Front.

Design by Ruby Thacker.

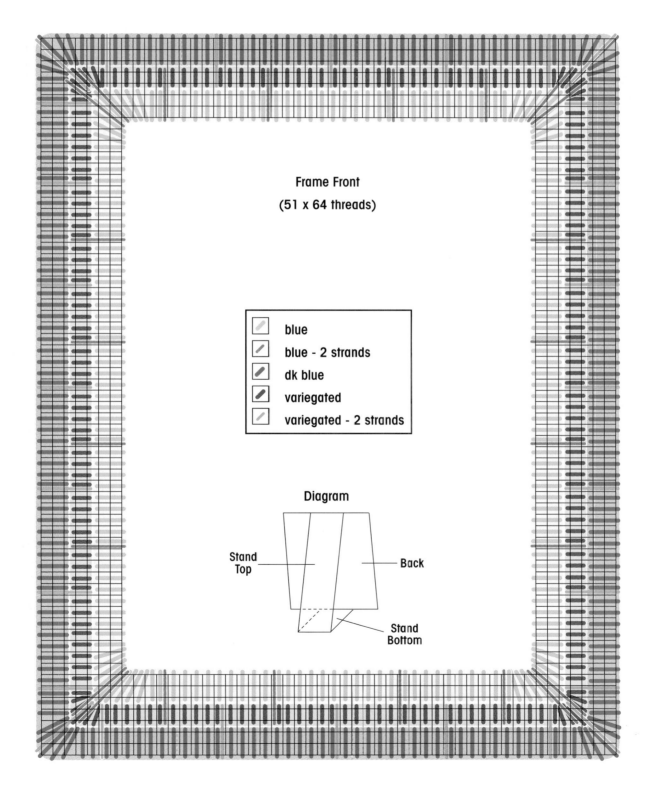

Frame Front
(51 x 64 threads)

	blue
	blue - 2 strands
	dk blue
	variegated
	variegated - 2 strands

Diagram

Stand Top — Back

Stand Bottom

SOUTHWESTERN COASTERS

(Shown on page 33)

Approx. Size: $5\frac{1}{4}$"w x $5\frac{1}{4}$"h each

Supplies: Worsted weight yarn, two Uniek® 5" hexagon shapes, one Uniek® 5" star shape, #16 tapestry needle, cork or felt (optional), and craft glue (optional)

Stitches Used: Backstitch, Gobelin Stitch, Overcast Stitch, and Tent Stitch

Instructions: For Coaster #1 only, follow chart to cut one hexagon shape. Follow charts to stitch Coasters. Using matching color yarn, cover unworked edges of Coasters.

If desired, cut a piece of cork or felt slightly smaller than each Coaster. Glue cork or felt to back of Coasters.

Designs by Ann Townsend.

✎	lt rose	✎	dk blue
✎	rose	✎	lt green
✎	lt blue	✎	green
✎	blue		

Coaster #1

Coaster #2

Coaster #3

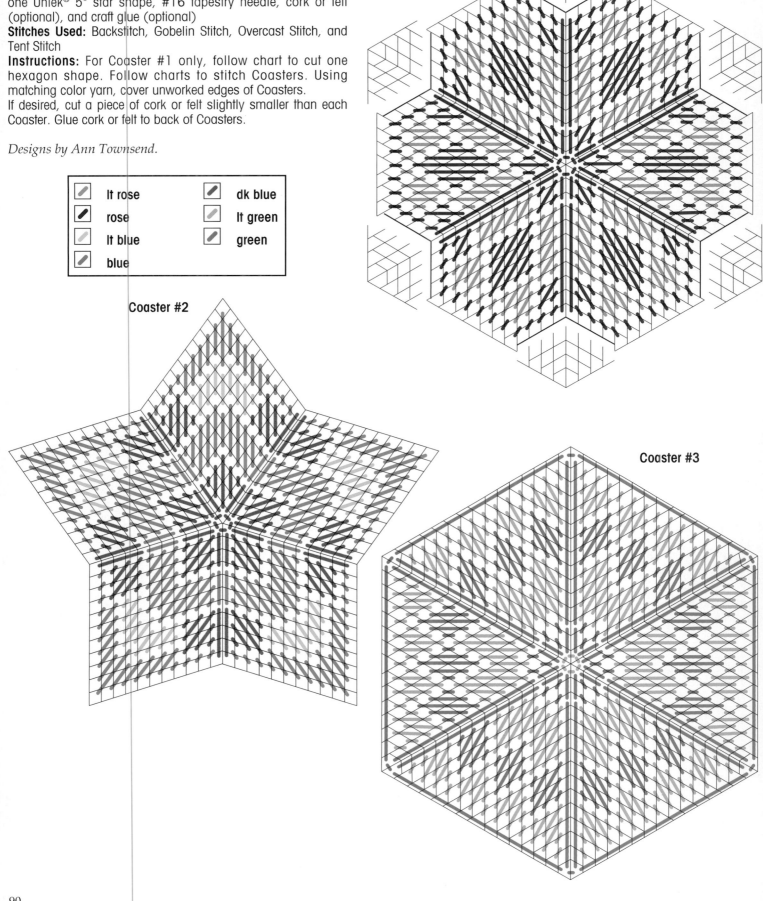

90

GENERAL INSTRUCTIONS
SELECTING PLASTIC CANVAS

Plastic canvas is a molded, nonwoven canvas made from clear or colored plastic. The canvas consists of "threads" and "holes." The threads aren't actually "threads" since the canvas is nonwoven, but it seems to be an accurate description of the straight lines of the canvas. The holes, as you would expect, are the spaces between the threads. The threads are often referred to in the project instructions, especially when cutting out plastic canvas pieces. The instructions for stitches will always refer to holes when explaining where to place your needle to make a stitch.

Types of Canvas. The main difference between types of plastic canvas is the mesh size. Mesh size refers to the number of holes in one inch of canvas. The most common mesh sizes are 5 mesh, 7 mesh, 10 mesh, and 14 mesh. Five mesh means that there are 5 holes in every inch of canvas. Likewise, there are 7 holes in every inch of 7 mesh canvas, 10 holes in every inch of 10 mesh canvas, and 14 holes in every inch of 14 mesh canvas. Seven mesh canvas is the most popular size for the majority of projects.

Your project supply list will tell you what size mesh you need to buy. Be sure to use the mesh size the project instructions recommend. If your project calls for 7 mesh canvas and you use 10 mesh, your finished project will be much smaller than expected. For example, suppose your instructions tell you to use 7 mesh canvas to make a boutique tissue box cover. You will need to cut each side 30 x 38 threads so they will measure $4^1/2$" x $5^3/4$" each. But if you were using 10 mesh canvas your sides would only measure 3" x $3^7/8$"! Needless to say, your tissue box cover from 10 mesh canvas would not fit a boutique tissue box.

Most plastic canvas is made from clear plastic, but colored canvas is also available. Colored plastic is ideal when you don't want to stitch the entire background.

When buying canvas, you may find that some canvas is firm and rigid, while other canvas is softer and more pliable. To decide which type of canvas is right for your project, think of how the project will be used. If you are making a box or container, you will want to use firmer canvas so that the box will be sturdy and not buckle after handling. If you are making a tissue box cover, you will not need the firmer canvas because the tissue box will support the

canvas and prevent warping. Softer canvas is better for projects that require a piece of canvas to be bent before it is joined to another piece.

Amount of Canvas. The project supply list usually tells you how much canvas you will need to complete the project. When buying your canvas, remember that several different manufacturers produce plastic canvas. Therefore, there are often slight variations in canvas, such as different thicknesses of threads or a small difference in mesh size. Because of these variations, try to buy enough canvas for your entire project at the same time and place. As a general rule, it is always better to buy too much canvas and have leftovers than to run out of canvas before you finish your project. By buying a little extra canvas, you not only allow for mistakes, but have extra canvas for practicing your stitches. Scraps of canvas are also excellent for making magnets and other small projects.

SELECTING YARN

You're probably thinking, "How do I select my yarn from the thousands of choices available?" Well, we have a few hints to help you choose the perfect yarns for your project and your budget.

Yarn Weight. We used various brands of worsted weight yarn to stitch some of the photography models for this book. You may wish to use Needloft® Plastic Canvas Yarn in place of the worsted weight yarn. To help you select colors for your projects, we have included numbers for Needloft yarn in some of our color keys. Needloft yarn is suitable only for 7 mesh plastic canvas. Refer to Types of Yarn, page 92, for additional information.

Yarn Cost. Cost may also be a factor in your yarn selection. Again, acrylic yarn is a favorite because it is reasonably priced and comes in a wide variety of colors. However, if your project is something extra special, you may want to spend a little more on tapestry yarn or Persian wool yarn to get certain shades of color.

Dye Lot Variations. It is important to buy all of the yarn you need to complete your project from the same dye lot. Although variations in color may be slight when yarns from two different dye lots are held together, the variation is usually apparent on a stitched piece.

Embroidery Floss. Embroidery floss consists of six strands that are twisted together. To ensure smoother stitches, separate the strands of floss and realign them before threading your needle. Refer to

the color key or project instructions for the number of strands to use for each project.

Yarn Colors. Choosing colors can be fun, but sometimes a little difficult. Your project will tell you what yarn colors you will need. When you begin searching for the recommended colors, you may be slightly overwhelmed by the different shades of each color. Here are a few guidelines to consider when choosing your colors.

Consider where you are going to place the finished project. If the project is going in a particular room in your house, match your yarn to the room's colors.

Try not to mix very bright colors with dull colors. For example, if you're stitching a project using country colors, don't use a bright Christmas red with country blues and greens. Instead, use a maroon or country red. Likewise, if you are stitching a bright tissue box cover for a child's room, don't use country blue with bright red, yellow, and green.

Some projects require several shades of a color, such as shades of pink for a flower. Be sure your shades blend well together.

Sometimes, you may have trouble finding three or four shades of a color. If you think your project warrants the extra expense, you can usually find several shades of a color available in tapestry yarn or Persian wool yarn.

Remember, you don't have to use the colors suggested in the color key. If you find a red tissue box cover that you really like, but your house is decorated in blue, change the colors in the tissue box cover to blue!

Yarn Yardage Estimator. A handy way of estimating yardage is to make a yarn yardage estimator. Cut a one-yard piece of yarn for each different stitch used in your project. For each stitch, work as many stitches as you can with the one-yard length of yarn.

To use your yarn yardage estimator, count the number of stitches you were able to make, suppose 72 Tent Stitches. Now look at the chart for the project you want to make. Estimate the number of ecru Tent Stitches on the chart, suppose 150. Now divide the estimated number of ecru stitches by the actual number stitched with a yard of yarn. One hundred fifty divided by 72 is approximately two. So you will need about two yards of ecru yarn to make your project. Repeat this for all stitches and yarn colors. To allow for repairs and practice

Continued on page 92

stitches, purchase extra yardage of each color. If you have yarn left over, remember that scraps of yarn are perfect for small projects such as magnets or when you need just a few inches of a particular color for another project.

TYPES OF YARN

Yarn Usage. The first question to ask when choosing yarn is, "How will my project be used?" If your finished project will be handled or used a lot, such as a coaster or magnet, you will want to use a durable, washable yarn. We highly recommend acrylic or nylon yarn for plastic canvas. It can be washed repeatedly and holds up well to frequent usage and handling. If your finished project won't be handled or used frequently, such as a framed picture or a bookend, you are not limited to washable yarns.

The types of yarns available are endless, and each grouping of yarn has its own characteristics and uses. The following is a brief description of some common yarns used for plastic canvas.

Worsted Weight Yarn. This yarn may be found in acrylic, wool, wool blends, and a variety of other fiber contents. Worsted weight yarn is the most popular yarn used for 7 mesh plastic canvas because one strand covers the canvas very well. This yarn is inexpensive and comes in a wide range of colors.

Most brands of worsted weight yarn have four plies that are twisted together to form one strand. When the color key indicates "2-ply," separate the strand of yarn and stitch using only two of the four plies.

Needloft® Yarn will not easily separate. When the instructions call for "2-ply" yarn, we recommend that you substitute with six strands of embroidery floss.

Sport Weight Yarn. This yarn has four thin plies that are twisted together to form one strand. Like worsted weight yarn, sport weight yarn comes in a variety of fiber contents. The color selection in sport weight yarn is more limited than in other types of yarns. You may want to use a double strand of sport weight yarn for better coverage of your 7 mesh canvas. Sport weight yarn works nicely for 10 mesh canvas.

Tapestry Yarn. This is a thin wool yarn.

Because tapestry yarn is available in a wider variety of colors than other yarns, it may be used when several shades of the same color are desired. For example, if you need five shades of pink to stitch a flower, you may choose tapestry yarn for a better blending of colors. Tapestry yarn is ideal for working on 10 mesh canvas. However, it is a more expensive yarn and requires two strands to cover 7 mesh canvas. Projects made with tapestry yarn cannot be washed.

Persian Wool. This is a wool yarn that is made up of three loosely twisted plies. The plies should be separated and realigned before you thread your needle. Like tapestry yarn, Persian yarn has more shades of each color from which to choose. It also has a nap similar to the nap of velvet. To determine the direction of the nap, run the yarn through your fingers. When you rub "with the nap," the yarn feels smooth; but when you rub "against the nap," the yarn feels rough. For smoother and prettier stitches on your project, stitching should be done "with the nap." The yarn fibers will stand out when stitching is done "against the nap." Because of the wool content, you cannot wash projects made with Persian yarn.

Pearl Cotton. Sometimes #3 pearl cotton is used on plastic canvas to give it a dressy, lacy look. It is not meant to cover 7 mesh canvas completely but to enhance it. Pearl cotton works well on 10 mesh canvas when you want your needlework to have a satiny sheen. If you cannot locate #3 pearl cotton in your area, you can substitute with 12 strands of embroidery floss.

SELECTING NEEDLES

Stitching on plastic canvas should be done with a blunt needle called a tapestry needle. Tapestry needles are sized by numbers; the higher the number, the smaller the needle. The correct size needle to use depends on the canvas mesh size and the yarn thickness. The needle should be small enough to allow the threaded needle to pass through the canvas holes easily, without disturbing canvas threads. The eye of the needle should be large enough to allow yarn to be threaded easily. If the eye is too small, the yarn will wear thin and may break. You will find the recommended needle size listed in the supply section of each project.

WORKING WITH PLASTIC CANVAS

Throughout this book, the lines of the canvas will be referred to as threads. However, they are not actually "threads" since the canvas is nonwoven. To cut plastic canvas pieces accurately, count **threads** (not **holes**) as shown in **Fig. 1**.

Fig. 1

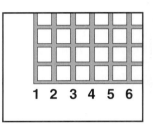

Thread Count. Before cutting your pieces, notice the thread count of each piece on your chart. The thread count is usually located above the piece on the chart. The thread count tells you the number of threads in the width and the height of the canvas piece. Follow the thread count to cut out a rectangle the specified size. Remember to count **threads**, not **holes**. If you accidentally count holes, your piece is going to be the wrong size. Follow the chart to trim the rectangle into the desired shape.

Marking the Canvas. If you find it necessary to mark on the canvas, use an overhead projector pen. Outline shape with pen, cut out shape, and remove markings with a damp paper towel.

Cutting the Canvas. A good pair of household scissors is recommended for cutting plastic canvas. However, a craft knife is helpful when cutting a small area from the center of a larger piece of canvas. For example, a craft knife is recommended for cutting the opening out of a tissue box cover top. When using a craft knife, be sure to protect the table below your canvas. A layer of cardboard or a magazine should provide enough padding to protect your table.

When cutting canvas, be sure to cut as close to the thread as possible without cutting into the thread. If you don't cut close enough, "nubs" or "pickets" will be left on the edge of your canvas. Be sure to cut all nubs from the canvas before you begin to stitch, because nubs will snag the yarn and are difficult to cover.

When cutting plastic canvas along a diagonal, cut through the center of each intersection. This will leave enough plastic canvas on both sides of the cut so that both pieces of canvas may be used. Diagonal corners will also snag yarn less and be easier to cover.

If your project has several pieces, you may want to cut them all out before you begin stitching. Keep your cut pieces in a resealable plastic bag to prevent loss.

THREADING YOUR NEEDLE
Many people wonder, "What is the best way to thread my needle?" Here are a couple of methods. Practice each one with a scrap of yarn and see what works best for you. There are also several yarn-size needle threaders available at your local craft store.

Fold Method. First, sharply fold the end of yarn over your needle; then remove needle. Keeping the fold sharp, push the needle onto the yarn **(Fig. 2)**.

Fig. 2

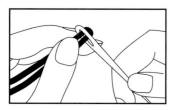

Thread Method. Fold a 5" piece of sewing thread in half, forming a loop. Insert loop of thread through the eye of your needle **(Fig. 3)**. Insert yarn through the loop and pull the thread back through your needle, pulling yarn through at the same time.

Fig. 3

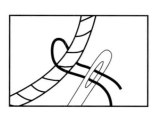

READING THE COLOR KEY
A color key is included for each project. The key indicates the colors of yarn used and how each color is represented on the chart. For example, when white yarn is represented by a grey line in the color key, all grey stitches on the chart should be stitched using white yarn.

READING THE CHART
Whenever possible, the drawing on the chart looks like the completed stitch. For example, the Tent Stitches on the chart are drawn diagonally across one intersection of threads just like Tent Stitches look on your piece of canvas. Likewise, Gobelin Stitches on the chart look identical to the Gobelin Stitches on your canvas. When a stitch cannot clearly be drawn on the chart, such as a French Knot, a symbol will be used instead. If you have difficulty determining how a particular stitch is worked, refer to Stitch Diagrams, page 94.

STITCHING THE DESIGN
Securing the First Stitch. Don't knot the end of your yarn before you begin stitching. Instead, begin each length of yarn by coming up from the wrong side of the canvas and leaving a 1" - 2" tail on the wrong side. Hold this tail against the canvas and work the first few stitches over the tail. When thread is secure, clip the tail close to your stitched piece. Clipping the tail closely is important because long tails can become tangled in future stitches or show through to the right side of the canvas.

Using Even Tension. Keep your stitching tension consistent, with each stitch lying flat and even on the canvas. Pulling or yanking the yarn causes the tension to be too tight, and you will be able to see through your project. Loose tension is caused by not pulling the yarn firmly enough, and the yarn will not lie flat on the canvas.

Ending Your Stitches. After you've completed all of the stitches of one color in an area, end your stitching by running your needle under several stitches on the back of the stitched piece. To keep the tails of the yarn from showing through or becoming tangled in future stitches, trim the end of the yarn close to the stitched piece.

Stitching Tips
Length of Yarn. It is best to begin stitching with a piece of yarn that is approximately one yard long. However, when working large areas of the same color, you may want to begin with a longer length of yarn to reduce the number of yarn ends and keep the back of your project looking neat.

Keeping Stitches Smooth. Most stitches tend to twist the yarn. Drop your needle and let the yarn untwist every few stitches or whenever needed.

JOINING PIECES
Straight Edges. The most common method of assembling stitched pieces is joining two or more pieces of canvas along a straight edge using Overcast Stitches. Place one piece on top of the other with right or wrong sides together. Make sure the edges being joined are even, then stitch the pieces together through all layers.

Shaded Areas. The shaded area is part of a chart that has colored shading on top of it. Shaded areas usually mean that all the stitches in that area are used to join pieces of canvas. Do not work the stitches in a shaded area until your project instructions say you should.

Stacking. Sometimes pieces need to be thicker than one layer of canvas. You can do this by stacking. Before you begin stitching, follow your project instructions to stack together plastic canvas pieces so that the edges are even.

Tacking. To tack pieces, run your needle under the backs of some stitches on one stitched piece to secure the yarn. Then run your needle through the canvas or under the stitches on the piece to be tacked in place. The idea is to securely attach your pieces without your tacking stitches showing.

Uneven Edges. Sometimes you'll need to join a diagonal edge to a straight edge. The holes of the two pieces will not line up exactly. Just keep the pieces even and stitch through holes as many times as necessary to completely cover the canvas.

Unworked Threads. Sometimes you'll need to join the edge of one piece to an unworked thread in the center of another piece. Simply place one piece on top of the other, matching the indicated threads or symbols. Join by stitching through both layers.

WASHING INSTRUCTIONS
If you used washable yarn for all of your stitches, you may hand-wash plastic canvas projects in warm water with a mild soap. Do not rub or scrub stitches; this will cause the yarn to fuzz. Allow your stitched piece to air dry. Do not put stitched pieces in a clothes dryer. The plastic canvas could melt in the heat of a dryer. Do not dry clean your plastic canvas. The chemicals used in dry cleaning could dissolve the plastic canvas. When piece is dry, you may need to trim the fuzz from your project with a small pair of sharp scissors.

Continued on page 94

STITCH DIAGRAMS

> **Unless otherwise indicated, bring threaded needle up at 1 and all odd numbers and down at 2 and all even numbers.**

ALTERNATING SCOTCH STITCH

This Scotch Stitch variation is worked over three or more threads, forming alternating blocks **(Fig. 4)**.

Fig. 4

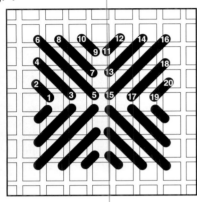

BACKSTITCH

This stitch is worked over completed stitches to outline or define **(Fig. 5)**. It is sometimes worked over more than one thread. Backstitch may also be used to cover canvas as shown in **Fig. 6**.

Fig. 5

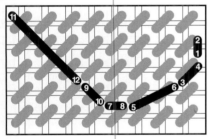

Fig. 6

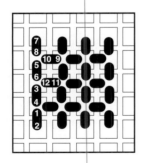

BRAIDED CROSS STITCH

This stitch covers the edge of the canvas. Begin by working stitches 1 through 3 **(Fig. 7)**. Starting with 4, proceed to work stitches in **Fig. 8** and **Fig. 9**, working forward over three threads and back over two. It may be necessary to work extra stitches at corners for better coverage.

Fig. 7

Fig. 8

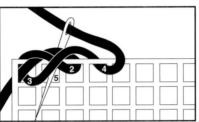

Fig. 9

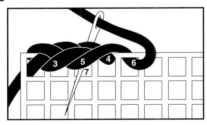

CROSS STITCH

This stitch is composed of two stitches **(Fig. 10)**. The top stitch of each cross must always be made in the same direction. The number of intersections may vary according to the chart.

Fig. 10

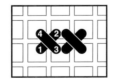

FRENCH KNOT

Bring needle up through hole. Wrap yarn once around needle and insert needle in same hole or adjacent hole, holding end of yarn with non-stitching fingers **(Fig. 11)**. Tighten knot; then pull needle through canvas, holding yarn until it must be released.

Fig. 11

FRINGE STITCH

Fold a length of yarn in half. Thread needle with loose ends of yarn. Bring needle up at 1, leaving a 1" loop on the back of the canvas. Bring needle around the edge of canvas and through loop **(Fig. 12)**. Pull to tighten loop **(Fig. 13)**. Trim strands to desired length from knot. A dot of glue on back of Fringe will help keep stitches in place.

Fig. 12

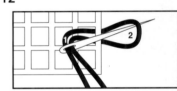

Fig. 13

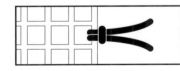

GOBELIN STITCH

This basic straight stitch is worked over two or more threads or intersections. The number of threads or intersections may vary according to the chart **(Fig. 14)**.

Fig. 14

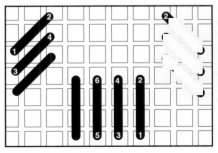

MODIFIED EYELET STITCH

This stitch forms a square over three threads of canvas. It consists of seven stitches worked in a clockwise or counterclockwise fashion. Each stitch is worked from the outer edge into the same central hole **(Fig. 15)**.

Fig. 15

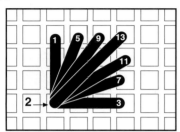

MOSAIC STITCH

This three-stitch pattern forms small squares **(Fig. 16)**.

Fig. 16

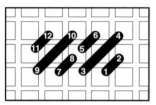

OVERCAST STITCH

This stitch covers the edge of the canvas and joins pieces of canvas **(Fig. 17)**. It may be necessary to go through the same hole more than once to get an even coverage on the edge, especially at the corners.

Fig. 17

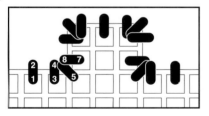

Instructions tested and photography items made by Janet Akins, Toni Bowden, Sharla Dunigan, Michelle E. Goodrich, Carlene Hodge, Gary Hutcheson, Patricia McCauley, and Sadie Wilson.

PADDED SATIN STITCH

This stitch is worked in two steps. First, work horizontal stitches as shown in **Fig. 18**. Then work vertical stitches over the horizontal stitches **(Fig. 19)**.

Fig. 18

Fig. 19

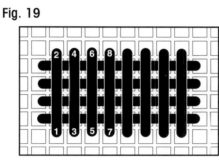

SCOTCH STITCH

This stitch forms a square. It may be worked over three or more horizontal threads by three or more vertical threads. **Fig. 20** shows the Scotch Stitch worked over three threads.

Fig. 20

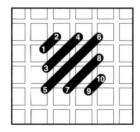

SMYRNA CROSS STITCH

This stitch is worked over two threads as a decorative stitch. Each stitch is worked completely before going on to the next **(Fig. 21)**.

Fig. 21

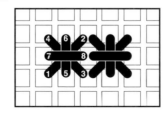

TENT STITCH

This stitch is worked in horizontal or vertical rows over one intersection as shown in **Fig. 22**. Follow **Fig. 23** to work the **Reversed Tent Stitch**. Sometimes when you are working Tent Stitches, the last stitch on the row will look "pulled" on the front of your piece when you are changing directions. To avoid this problem, leave a loop of yarn on the wrong side of the stitched piece after making the last stitch in the row. When making the first stitch in the next row, run your needle through the loop **(Fig. 24)**. Gently pull yarn until all stitches are even.

Fig. 22

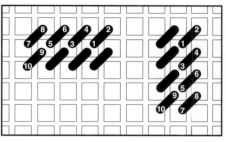

Fig. 23

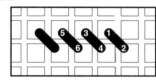

Fig. 24

TURKEY LOOP STITCH

This stitch is composed of locked loops. Bring needle up through hole and back down through same hole, forming a loop on top of the canvas. A locking stitch is then made across the thread directly below or to either side of loop as shown in **Fig. 25**.

Fig. 25

INDEX